Lab Manual
for
Boctor's
Electric Circuit
Analysis

Second Edition

Mohamed Ghorab
Shiva Prabhu

Ryerson Polytechnic University

LAB MARKS.

20%.

8 MARKS
lab Quizes
+
attendance

12 MARKS
Final lab test (individual)

M TAM (JIAL YIN)
1701042?1 (905)

ARTURO WONG Crt,

CONTENTS

PREFACE

The important objective of any laboratory session is to
reinforce the understanding and the use of theoretical
background through first hand experience with relevant
experiments and calculations. This laboratory text is
written with the primary goal of addressing the above
objective and as well to provide the student with the skills
needed in using the equipment properly.

The experiments covered in the text are designed to
complement the text "Electric Circuit Analysis" by Dr. S.A.
Boctor. They have been developed and tested over the past
few years at the authors' institute and proven to be
effective in aiding the students in better understanding of
the basic concepts in Electric Circuit Theory.

Each of the above experiments begins with a reference to a
specific chapter and section in the text book, followed by a
prelab assignment related to the objectives of the
experiment and is meant to to enhance the students'
appreciation of theory versus practice. The experimental
procedure is written in "steps-format" accompanied by
appropriate tables and graphs. This format allows the
student more time to examine the experimental data and
analyze the results. Each experiment concludes with a set of
questions designed to achieve a better understanding of the
concepts examined.

This laboratory text is readily adaptable in a two-semester
course in Electric Circuit Analysis.

We are grateful to our colleagues at our institute for their
sugestions and help in improving the laboratory text over
the years. especially to Professor John Van Arragon, whose
work has provided the necessary basis for many of these
experiments.

Our appreciation also goes to the reviewers of this manual--
Vincent Loizzo-DeVry Institute of Technology, Chicago, IL,
A. David Nawricki-Texas State Technical Institute,
Sweetwater, TX, and Philip Regalbuto-Trident Technical
College, Charleston, SC.

INTRODUCTION TO ELECTRICAL MEASUREMENT

0.1   Definition of Terms:

In making measurements (voltage, current, resistance, etc.), we employ a number of terms which need to be accurately defined.

These terms are:

a)   Sensitivity: "a measure of the smallest quantity (voltage, current, etc.) that will produce an observable deflection" (using deflection-type instrument).

b)   Accuracy: "the degree to which the measured value approaches the true value", usually expressed as a percentage of full-scale deflection (fsd). For example, a voltmeter with a fsd of 100V may have its accuracy stated as $\pm$ 2%. When the pointer of this voltmeter indicates 50V, the actual measured voltage must be taken as 50V $\pm$ 2% of fsd, i.e. the measured voltage is somewhere between 48V and 52V.

c)   Precision: "the degree to which a measurement is sharply defined", expressed by the number of significant figures in the reading. It is also defined as the smallest measurable difference between two readings.

d)   Linearity: "the degree to which a graph of the actual value of measured quantity, versus the reading of the instrument, deviates from an ideal straight line drawn between the end points of the actual curve", as shown in Fig. 0.1

1

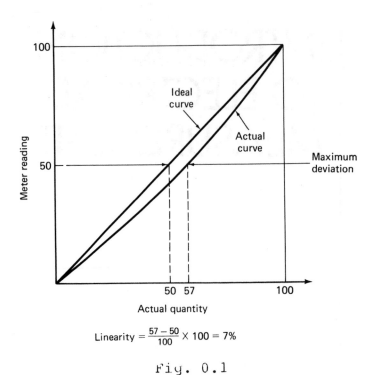

$$\text{Linearity} = \frac{57 - 50}{100} \times 100 = 7\%$$

Fig. 0.1

0.2   Measurement Pitfalls:

Here are a number of tips for interpreting measured data:-

a)   Meter accuracy is usually specified by the allowable error as a percentage of fsd. Thus, a reading of 15V, on the 100V $\pm$ 2% scale, must be interpreted as having the limits of 15 $\pm$ 2V or 15V $\pm$ 13.3%. Obviously, for the greatest measurement accuracy, the best range to use is the one that gives the largest deflection, not exceeding the fsd (full-scale deflection).

b)   Meter calibration often changes abruptly with range changes, without any actual change in the measured quantity taking place. Therefore, whenever a string of readings is to be taken, it may be wise to take all readings using the same range.

c)   Beware of subtracting two almost equal pieces of data. The uncertainty associated with each reading can make the result of subtraction almost meaningless. For example, 40V and 45V readings on a 100 $\pm$ 2% scale could be either (47-38) = 9V or (43-42) = 1V; the ideal result, however, is 5V. It can be easily shown that the limits of the error here are $\pm$ 80%.

0.3   Reading of Deflection-Type Meter:

$$\text{The meter reading} = \text{Range} \times \frac{\text{Deflection}}{\text{fsd}}$$

2

Example 0.1

Determine the reading of the multimeter, shown in Fig. 0.2, for each position of the range selector.

Range Selector Position:

a - 10V
b - 250V
c - 100 μ A
d - 50 mA

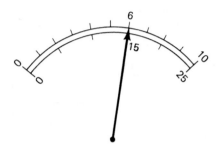

Fig. 0.2

0.4   Current Measurement:

The instrument used to measure electric current is called an "ammeter." Ignoring its internal components, a deflection-type DC ammeter consists basically of: a calibrated (linear) scale over which a pointer is deflected to indicate the measured current, two terminals identified by a + and -, and a range switch to select the current range of each particular measurement.

An ammeter must be connected so that the current to be measured flows through the meter. Consequently, AMMETERS ARE ALWAYS CONNECTED IN SERIES WITH THE COMPONENT IN WHICH THE CURRENT IS TO BE MEASURED, as shown in Figure 0.3.

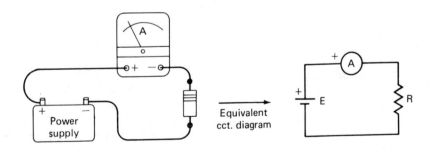

Fig 0.3

0.5   Voltage Measurement:

The instrument used to measure the voltage _difference_ between two points in an electric circuit is called a "voltmeter." The basic deflection-type DC voltmeter is similar in appearance to an ammeter, i.e., the instrument has a + and - terminal, a range switch, and a pointer which moves over a linearly-calibrated scale in volts.

VOLTMETERS ARE ALWAYS CONNECTED IN PARALLEL WITH THE CIRCUIT-NODES ACROSS WHICH THE VOLTAGE DIFFERENCE IS TO BE MEASURED, as shown in Figure 0.4.

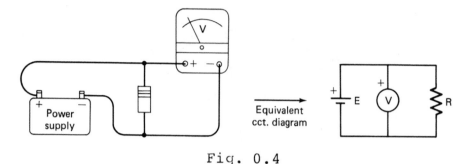

Fig. 0.4

0.6   Resistance Measurement:

Resistance is measured by means of an "ohmmeter." The Ohmmeter has its own internal DC source for the purpose of passing a current through the resistance to be measured. The resulting current (which is inversely proportional to the resistance) causes the pointer to move over a nonlinearly-calibrated scale in ohms. Notice that the ohmmeter scale is quite different from that on the other meters: it is nonlinear; zero deflection corresponds to infinite ohms, and full-scale deflection (fsd) corresponds to zero ohms.

AN OHMMETER MUST NEVER BE CONNECTED TO ANY PART OF AN EXTERNALLY-ENERGIZED CIRCUIT.

The Ohmmeter measures resistance most accurately when its pointer position is around the mid-scale range.

0.7   Hints for Plotting Graphs:

a)   Selection of axes: To plot a graph representing the relationship between two variables, one must have a clear idea as to which of the two variables is considered independent (cause), and which is dependent (effect). The x-axis is then selected to represent the cause, while the y-axis represents the effect. In current (I) _versus_ voltage (V) graph, current is dependent on the magnitude of the voltage, i.e. voltage is the cause for the current (effect) to flow.

b)   Selection of Observation points: With unlimited time
      and energy at hand, one might consider taking many
      observations (measurements) to plot a graph; the more
      observations taken, the more accurate is the resulting
      graph.   However, for a limited number of observations,
      n, we wish to select the observation values along the
      cause-axis (x-axis) at which we take our measurements
      of the effect (y-axis), and which also provides optimum
      graph accuracy.   Our choice will depend on the width of
      the range of values of "x" over which we wish to
      measure "y."

      (1)   Linear-scale: for a narrow range of values
             of cause variations, we usually choose a
             linear scale along the x-axis.   The distance,
             d, between successive observation points is
             selected as:

      d = [highest value of "x" - lowest value of "x"] / (n-1)

Example 0.2

      Obtain the observation values along the x-
      axis that provide optimum graph accuracy.
      Given:

      $0 \leq x \leq 10$, and n = 6 points

Solution:

      d = (10-0)/(6-1) = 2

      Thus, the values of "x" are: 0, 2, 4, 6, 8, & 10.

      (2)   Logarithmic (non-linear)-scale: For a wide
             range of values of cause variation, we
             usually choose a logarithmic scale along the
             x-axis.

      The ratio of two successive observation
      points, r, is selected as:

      $r = [\text{highest value of "x"/lowest value of "x"}]^{\frac{1}{n-1}}$

Example 0.3

      Obtain the observation values along the x-
      axis that provide optimum graph accuracy.
      Given:

      $10 \leq x \leq 4000$, and n = 9 points

5

Solution:

$$r = [4000/10]^{(1/8)} = 2.11$$

Thus, the values of "x" are 10, 21, 45, 96, 200, 423, 894, 1891, & 4000.

0.8   Errors:

It is not possible to measure any quantity with perfect accuracy and as such, it is important to find out what the real accuracy is and how the different errors have entered into the measurements. A study of errors is important in finding ways to reduce them and also to estimate the reliability of the final result.

Errors can be classified as:

1)   Gross Errors
2)   Systematic Errors
3)   Random Errors

1)   Gross Errors: are largely due to human errors - mistakes in reading and recording of data, incorrect adjustment and improper application of instruments and mistakes in calculations.

These errors can only be avoided by taking care in reading and recording the measured data correctly.

CULTIVATE THE GOOD HABITS OF:

(a)   SELECTING THE PROPER SCALE AND RECORDING THE SCALE USED IN MEASUREMENTS.

(b)   ADJUSTING THE POINTER OF INSTRUMENT TO ZERO DEFLECTION BEFORE THE START OF THE EXPERIMENT.

(c)   DOUBLE CHECKING THE MEASUREMENTS BY YOU AND/OR YOUR PARTNER.

2)   Systematic Errors:

(a)   Instrumental Errors: are errors inherent in the instruments because of the tolerances and limits in the electrical and mechanical designs. Instrument errors can also be introduced due to misuse and loading effects of instruments. For example: a well-calibrated voltmeter may read erroneously when connected across two points in a high resistance circuit.

The above errors may be avoided by selecting a suitable instrument for the particular application, applying the proper correction factors once the amount of error is known.

> REMEMBER: CARELESS OR UNINFORMED USE OF AN INSTRUMENT MAY DO PERMANENT DAMAGE AS A RESULT OF OVER-LOADING AND OVERHEATING OF THE INSTRUMENT.

   (b) Environmental Errors: are errors due to external conditions to the measuring instrument due to changes in temperature, humidity, pressure or of magnetic or electrostatic fields. Corrective measures include the air-conditioning, use of magnetic shields, hermetically sealing certain components in the instrument etc.

   (c) Observational Errors: are errors introduced by the observer. An observer may tend to read higher (or lower) than the correct value, possibly because of his reading angle and failure to avoid parallax.

3) Random Errors: are errors due to unknown causes and occur even when all systematic errors have been taken into account. They become important in high-accuracy work. These unknown errors are probably caused by a large number of small, variable effects so that their cumulative effects may be negligible in some cases or have a large net positive or negative error introduced. The only way to offset these errors is by increasing the number of readings and using statistical analysis to obtain the best approximation of the true value.

NOTE: Most of the errors discussed can be avoided by the experimenter by proper usage of the instruments and in reading the instruments as accurately as possible.

It is important to discuss and comment on the accuracy of the reading obtained during the experimentation.

TABLE 2.3 STANDARD VALUES OF COMMERCIALLY AVAILABLE RESISTORS: 5% TOLERANCE[a]

Ohms (Ω)					Kilohms (kΩ)		Megohms (MΩ)	
0.10	**1.0**	**10**	**100**	**1000**	**10**	**100**	**1.0**	**10.0**
0.11	1.1	11	110	1100	11	110	1.1	11.0
0.12	**1.2**	**12**	**120**	**1200**	**12**	**120**	**1.2**	**12.0**
0.13	1.3	13	130	1300	13	130	1.3	13.0
0.15	**1.5**	**15**	**150**	**1500**	**15**	**150**	**1.5**	**15.0**
0.16	1.6	16	160	1600	16	160	1.6	16.0
0.18	**1.8**	**18**	**180**	**1800**	**18**	**180**	**1.8**	**18.0**
0.20	2.0	20	200	2000	20	200	2.0	20.0
0.22	**2.2**	**22**	**220**	**2200**	**22**	**220**	**2.2**	**22.0**
0.24	2.4	24	240	2400	24	240	2.4	
0.27	**2.7**	**27**	**270**	**2700**	**27**	**270**	**2.7**	
0.30	3.0	30	300	3000	30	300	3.0	
0.33	**3.3**	**33**	**330**	**3300**	**33**	**330**	**3.3**	
0.36	3.6	36	360	3600	36	360	3.6	
0.39	**3.9**	**39**	**390**	**3900**	**39**	**390**	**3.9**	
0.43	4.3	43	430	4300	43	430	4.3	
0.47	**4.7**	**47**	**470**	**4700**	**47**	**470**	**4.7**	
0.51	5.1	51	510	5100	51	510	5.1	
0.56	**5.6**	**56**	**560**	**5600**	**56**	**560**	**5.6**	
0.62	6.2	62	620	6200	62	620	6.2	
0.68	**6.8**	**68**	**680**	**6800**	**68**	**680**	**6.8**	
0.75	7.5	75	750	7500	75	750	7.5	
0.82	**8.2**	**82**	**820**	**8200**	**82**	**820**	**8.2**	
0.91	9.1	91	910	9100	91	910	9.1	

[a]**Boldface** figures are 10% values.

TABLE 2.4 COLOR CODING FOR CARBON-COMPOSITION RESISTORS

Color	First-band digit	Second-band digit	Third-band multiplier
Black	0	0	$10^0 = 1$
Brown	1	1	$10^1 = 10$
Red	2	2	$10^2 = 100$
Orange	3	3	$10^3 = 1000$
Yellow	4	4	$10^4 = 10\ 000$
Green	5	5	$10^5 = 100\ 000$
Blue	6	6	$10^6 = 1\ 000\ 000$
Violet	7	7	$10^7 = 10\ 000\ 000$
Gray	8	8	$10^8 = 100\ 000\ 000$
White	9	9	$10^9 = 1\ 000\ 000\ 000$
Gold			0.1
Silver			0.01

1 | SIMPLE DC CIRCUIT

Required Reading: Text, section 2.2 to 2.5

1.1   Objective:

- To become familiar with the use of meters.

- To plot and understand the I-V characteristics
  and power hyperbola contours of linear and
  non-linear resistors.

- To verify Ohm's law.

1.2   Prelab Assignment:

Consider the circuits shown in Fig. 1.1.

The I-V relationships for the load are as follows:

Load # 1 .... $I_1 = 2 \times 10^{-4} V_1$

Load # 2 .... $I_2 = 10^{-4} V_2$

Load # 3 .... $I_3 = 10^{-14} e^{+40V_3}$

9

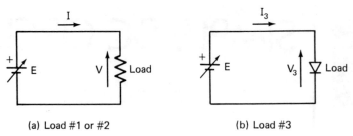

(a) Load #1 or #2   (b) Load #3

Fig. 1.1

(1) Determine the currents through loads 1 and 2 for the following values of voltages:

0, 5, 10, 15, 20, 25 volts

and plot the I-V characteristics of the loads on Graph 1.1.

(2) Determine the locus of points on the I-V characteristics of Graph 1.1 that represent a power dissipation of 50 mW. [Hint: calculate $I = \dfrac{(50 \text{ mW})}{V}$ mA for the values of the voltages suggested in (1)].

(3) Plot the I-V characteristics of load #3 on Graph 1.2 for a voltage range of 0 to 0.75 volts. Calculate, using the given I-V relationship, the resistance values at the following voltages and currents:

V = 0.5 volts,   V = 0.7 volts,

I = 1 mA,   I = 10 mA

$R = \frac{V}{I} = 0.5 M\Omega$ $0.07 m\Omega$

$V = I \cdot R.$

$I_3 = 10^{-14} \cdot e^{40 V_3}$

I	V
1.106	0.75
0.144	0.70
0.019	0.65

10

R = 2×10⁻⁴ LOAD #1

I	V
0	0
1.0×10⁻³	5
2.0×10⁻³	10
3.0×10⁻³	15
4.0×10⁻³	20
5.0×10⁻³	25

LOAD# 2. R = 10⁻⁴

I	V
0	0
5.0×10⁻³	5
0.01	10
0.015	15
0.02	20
0.025	25

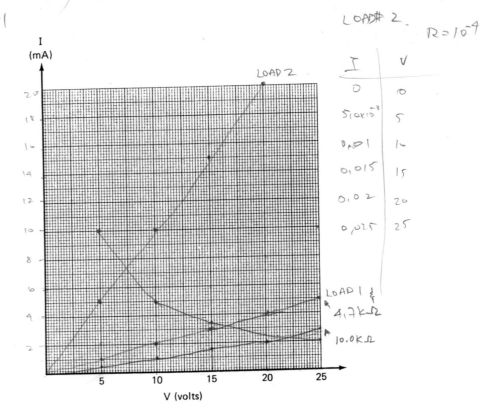

Graph 1.1

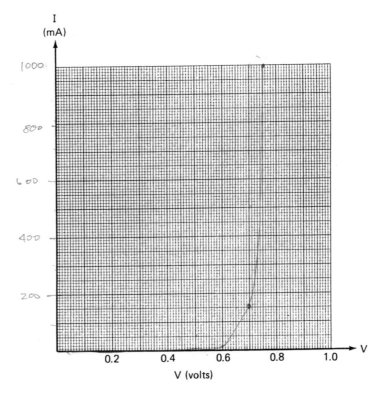

Graph 1.2

11

ITEM	MANUFACTURER AND MODEL NO.	LAB. SERIAL NO
DC Power Supply		
VOM		
DMM or milliammeter		

Resistors: One 4.7 kΩ and 10 kΩ .

1.4   **Procedure:**

A.   I-V Characteristics:

(1)   Connect the circuit shown in Fig 1.2
with R = 4.7 kΩ . 4700Ω

Y V$_R$

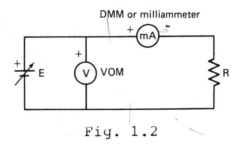

Fig. 1.2

(2)   Vary the applied voltage (E) from 0 to 25
volts. Measure the voltage (V) and
Current (I) values and record the results
in Table 1.1.

13

(3) Plot the I-V characteristic of the 4.7 kΩ resistor on Graph 1.1 using the experimental results.

(4) Repeat steps 1 and 2 with R = 10 kΩ ~~000 ohms~~ instead of 4.7 kΩ . Record your results in Table 1.1 and plot the I-V characteristic on Graph 1.1.

Table 1.1

R (kΩ) -nominal	VOLTMETER (V)		MILLIAMMETER (I)		OHM'S LAW $R=\dfrac{V}{I}$ kΩ	OHMMETER MEASUREMENT (kΩ)
	Range	Reading (Volts)	Range	Reading (mA)		
4.7	20✓	5	20m	1.06	4.716	4.7k.
	20	10	1)	2.12	4.716	
	20	15	1)	3.18	4.716	
	200	20	1)	4.26	4.694	
	200	25	1)	5.32	4.699	
10	20	5	20m	0.49	10.204	10.06k
	1)	10	1)	0.99	10.101	
		15		1.48	10.135	
	200	20	20	1.99	10.050	
	200	25		2.48	10.080	

B.   Resistance Measurements:

(1)   Set the VOM as an ohmmeter and select the
range-selector switch to X1 .

(2)   Short-circuit the ohmmeter terminals and
the meter should now show zero ohms or
full-scale deflection on the current
scale.   If the pointer is not at zero
ohms, adjust the potentiometer "ZERO"
till the pointer is at zero.   The meter
is now ready to be used as an ohmmeter.
(If the Ohm-range selector is switched to
another range, the zeroing procedure
should be followed for that range before
using the meter as an ohmmeter.)

(3)   Remove the short-circuit and connect the
resistor with the unknown value across
the ohmmeter terminals; the meter now
indicates the ohmic value of the
resistor.   Using the above procedure,
measure the ohmic values of the 4.7 kΩ
and the 10 kΩ resistors noting that the
R-scale is counterclockwise and non-
linear.   Record these values in Table
1.1.

(4)   If a DMM is used to measure the unknown
resistance value, set the meter on the

15

"resistance" mode of operation with the
proper range and measure the resistance.
Record the results in Table 1.1.

1.5   **Comments and Conclusions:**

1.   Determine the average value of the resistance
from the experimental I-V plot on Graph 1.1.

R (from I-V graph) = __4.7__ (nominal 4.7 kΩ

resistor)

= __10.06__ (nominal 10 kΩ

resistor)

2.   How do the above experimental values compare
with the nominal ratings and the measured
values using the ohmmeter?   Calculate the
percent errors using the relationship:

$$\% \ Error = \frac{[R(measured) \ - \ R(nominal)]}{R(nominal)} \ x \ 100$$

$$\frac{4.7 - 4.7}{4.7}, \ 100\%, \qquad \frac{10.06 - 10.00}{10.00} \cdot 100\%,$$

$$= 0\%, \qquad \qquad \qquad \sim \ 0.60\%,$$

3.   How is Ohm's law confirmed in this experiment?
Explain.

Voltage is proportional
to the current x resistance

4. What is the relationship between the magnitude of the resistance and the slope of the I-V characteristic?

    The magnitude of the resistance is the slope of the I-V graph.

5. Draw the I-V characteristics on Graph 1.1 of a resistor with:

    a)   R = O ohms

    b)   R = Infinite Value

6. What are the possible reasons for any errors or deviations in the results from the theoretical or nominal values? Explain.

    The current flow fluctuates all the time. The wires made and an increase of resistance.

2 | SERIES DC CIRCUIT

Required Reading: Text, section 3.4

2.1   Objective:

- To verify Kirchhoff's voltage law and other properties of a simple series DC circuit.

2.2   Prelab Assignment:

(1)   Consider the circuit shown in Fig. 2.1. The terminal voltage of the power supply is maintained at 25V.

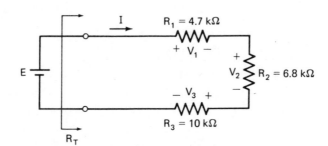

Fig. 2.1

Calculate:

(a) R_{Total}, I, $\dfrac{V_1}{E}$, $\dfrac{V_2}{V_3}$, $\dfrac{P_1}{P_T}$, $\dfrac{P_2}{P_3}$ $R_T = 21.5\,\Omega$ $I =$

(b) the maximum value of voltage that can be applied to the circuit without exceeding any of the component's power rating assuming that each resistor has a power rating of 1/2 watt.

Which resistor in this circuit is considered as the weakest link? Explain.

(2) Plot the I-V characteristics of R_1, R_2, R_3 and R_T on Graph 2.1.

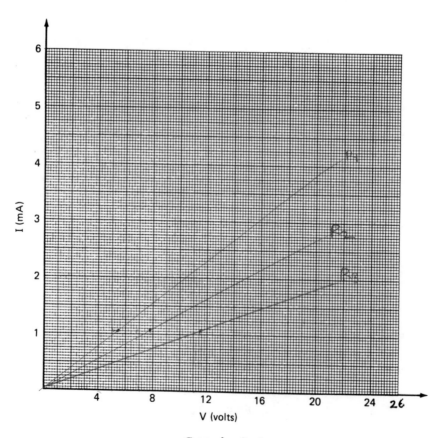

Graph 2.1

20

(3) What are the effects with respect to the voltage across, current through and power dissipation of each resistor, if the resistance of R_3 is increased? Record your answers in Table 2.1 using the following simple conventions:

'increase' ↑

'decrease' ↓

'no change' =

Table 2.1

COMP	R	V	I	P
R_1	=	↓	↓	↓
R_2	=	↓	↓	↓
R_3	↑	↓	↓	↑ ↓
TOTAL	↓	=	↓	↓

0,5W 4,7kΩ I 1/16mA

$$\frac{V^2}{R} = P$$

R_1

I | V

$$P = I^2 R$$
$$I = \sqrt{\frac{P}{R}}$$

$R_1 = 4.7 k\Omega, \frac{1}{2} W$; $\boxed{I_1 = 5mA}$ V_1

$R_2 = 6.8 k\Omega \frac{1}{2} W$ $I_2 = 10 m/A$ V_2

$R_3 = 10 k\Omega \frac{1}{2} W$ $I_3 = 7mA$ V_3

I_1 0.010 A

I_2 8.5mA

I_3 7.07mA

↑ MAX current.

Weakest resistor is $\underline{R_3}$

$R_T = 21500$

$V = I \cdot R$
$= 7.07mA \cdot 21500$
$= 152.07 V$

Prelab Work Space:

$R_T = R_1 + R_2 + R_3$ $E = V_T = 25v$ $V_1 = R_1 \cdot I_T$ $V_2 = R_2 \cdot I_e$

$\quad = 4.7 + 6.8 + 10$ $I_T = \dfrac{V_T}{R_T}$ $\quad = 4.7 \times 10^3 \cdot 1.16 \times 10^{-3}$ $\quad = 6.8 \times 10^3 (1.16 \times 10^{-3})$

$\quad = 21.5 k\Omega$ $\quad = 5.465 v$ $\quad = 7.91 v$

$\quad = 21500 \Omega$ $\quad = \dfrac{25}{21500}$

$\qquad\qquad\qquad\qquad \dfrac{V_1}{E} = \dfrac{5.465}{25} = 0.2186$ $V_3 = R_3 \cdot I_T$

$\qquad\qquad\qquad = 1.16 \times 10^{-3} A$ $\qquad\qquad\qquad\qquad\qquad = 10 \times 10^3 (1.16 \times 10^{-3})$

$\qquad\qquad\qquad\qquad\qquad\qquad\qquad\qquad\qquad = 11.63 v$

$\dfrac{P_1}{P_T} = \dfrac{I_T^2 R_1}{I_T^2 (R_T)} = \dfrac{(1.16 \times 10^{-3})^2 \cdot 4.7 \times 10^3}{(1.6 \times 10^{-3})^2 \cdot 21.5 \times 10^3}$ $\dfrac{V_2}{V_3} = \dfrac{7.91 v}{11.63 v} = 0.6802.$

$\qquad\qquad = \dfrac{4.7 \times 10^3}{21.5 \times 10^3}$

$\qquad\qquad = 0.286.$

$\dfrac{P_2}{P_3} = \dfrac{I_T^2 R_2}{I_T^2 R_3} = \dfrac{R_2}{R_3} = \dfrac{6.8}{10} = 0.68$

	R_1		R_2		R_3	
I_T	V		I_c	V	I_c	V
7.16×10^{-3}	5.482		1.16×10^{-3}	7.88	1.16×10^{-3}	11.6

$P = \dfrac{V^2}{R}$

$R = \dfrac{V^2}{P} = \dfrac{(V_1)^2}{P} = \dfrac{(5.465)^2}{0.5} = 1093 \Omega$ $4.700 \quad 3607$

$\qquad = \dfrac{V_2^2}{P} = \dfrac{(7.91)^2}{0.5} = 125.1362$ $6800 = 6674.86$

$\qquad = \dfrac{U_s^2}{P} = \dfrac{(11.63)^2}{0.5} = 27052$ $10000 = 97292 \Omega$

$\therefore$ weakest least er

$P_e = \dfrac{U^2}{R}$ $0.5 = \dfrac{V^2}{21500}$ R_3

$\qquad\qquad\qquad V = 103.68 v$

2.3   Equipment:

ITEM	MANUFACTURER AND MODEL NO.	LAB. SERIAL NO
DC Power Supply		
VOM		
DMM or DC milliammeter		

Resistors: One 4.7 kΩ , 6.8 kΩ , 10 kΩ , 15kΩ

2.4   Procedure:

(1)   Connect the circuit shown in Fig. 2.2.

The terminal voltage of the power supply is to be set at 25V while the circuit is connected.

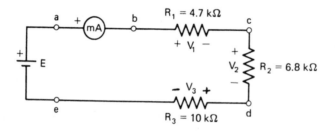

Fig. 2.2

(2)   Measure the applied voltage (E), V_1, V_2 and V_3 and the current supplied from source (I_T). Record the results in Table 2.2.

(3)   Disconnect the milliammeter from its present location and connect the meter at the proper locations in the above circuit to measure the

24

currents through R_1, R_2, and R_3 respectively. Record
your results in Table 2.2.

$\rho = I^2 \cdot R$.

Table 2.2

Component	VOLTMETER		MILLIAMMETER		R (calculated) $= (\dfrac{volts}{mA}) \, k\Omega$	Power (calculated) mW
	Range	Reading (Volts)	Range	Reading (mA)		
DC POWER SUPPLY		25		1.16 mA	$R_T = 21.55 \, k\Omega$	28.99 mW
R_1	200	5.4	20	1.16 m A	$R_1 = 4.655 \, k\Omega$	6.26 mW
R_2	200	7.9		1.16m A	$R_2 = 6.810 \, k\Omega$	9.16 mW
R_3	200	11.6		1.16 m A	$R_3 = 10 \, k\Omega$	13.456 mW

24.9

(4) Calculate the values of R_T, R_1, R_2 and R_3 and
the power in each resistor from the voltage
and current measurements. Record these values
in Table 2.2. Plot the I-V characteristics,
using the above readings, of all the resistors
on Graph 2.1. (The graph is exactly the same

(5) Compare the following quantities in Table 2.3
using the experimental values in Table 2.2:

Table 2.3

$V_1 + V_2 + V_3 = 24.9$ volts	$E = 25$ volts
$R_1 + R_2 + R_3 = 21.465$ kΩ	$R_T = 21.5$ kΩ
$\dfrac{V_1}{V_2} = 0.6835$	$\dfrac{R_1}{R_2} = 0.6835$
$\dfrac{V_3}{E} = 0.464$	$\dfrac{R_3}{R_T} = 0.4658$

(6) Replace R_3 in Fig 2.2 by a 15 kΩ resistor. Measure I_T, V_1, V_2, V_3 and E and record these values in Table 2.4. Calculate the power dissispated in each resistor and total power.

Table 2.4

E (V)	V_1 (V)	V_2 (V)	V_3 (V)	I_T (mA)	POWER = (VI_T) mW			
					P_1	P_2	P_3	P_T
25.1V	4.4 v	6.4N	14.1$V	0.94mA	4.13	6.016	13.25	23.59

How does the increase in the magnitude of R_3 affect the voltage across, current through and power dissipation of each resistor in the circuit? (Compare the results of Table 2.4 with the results in Table 2.2). Record these results in Table 2.1, using the

↑ , ↓ , = convention. [For clarity, use a

different color pencil or pen to emphasize the

experimental results.]

2.5   **Comments and Conclusions:**

1.   Summarize the properties of a DC series

circuit. Are these properties supported

by your experimental results? Use the

various data obtained in the experiments

to justify the statements.

- Current is the same throughout the entire circuit.
- If a path is broken, then entire circuit is broken.
- The total resistance is equal to the sum of all resistance.
- The total potential energy is equal to the sum of each potential energy.

$P = I^2 R$ — an increase of resistance will cause the total current and voltage to decrease.

2. What are the possible causes for any
   deviations in the experimental results from
   the theoretical or nominal values? Explain.

   — wires add more resistance to
   the circuit.
   — The % tolerance of each resistor

3. Is the Loading effect of VOM as the voltmeter
   significant in measuring the voltages in the
   circuit of Fig. 2.2? Explain.

   The voltmeter is thought ideally as
   an open circuit in which $R = \infty$
   However there is actually some resistance in
   althingh changes the measurement values.

4. What are the effects on I_T, V_1, V_2 and V_3
   if R_1, for some reason, is:

   (a) open-circuited;

   If R_1 is open circuit then
   there is no flow of current
   and therefore I_i, V_1, V_2 and V_3
   is equal to zero.

   (b) short-circuited?

   If R_1 is short circuit then the total
   resistance is less. The current
   will increase as for the
   voltages

$V = I \cdot R$

28

3 | PARALLEL DC CIRCUIT

Required Reading: Text, section 3.5

3.1   **Objective:**

To verify Kirchhoff's current law and other

properties of a parallel circuit.

3.2   **Prelab Assignment:**

(1)   Consider the circuit shown in Fig. 3.1.

The terminal voltage of the power supply is

maintained at 25V.

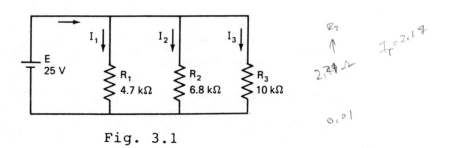

Fig. 3.1

Calculate:

(a) $R_T, G_T, I_T, \dfrac{I_1}{I_T}, \dfrac{I_2}{I_3}, \dfrac{G_1}{G_T}, \dfrac{G_2}{G_3}, \dfrac{P_1}{P_T}, \dfrac{P_2}{P_3}$

(b)   the maximum value of I_T that can be supplied to the circuit without exceeding any of the component's power rating, assuming that each resistor has a power rating of 1/2 watt.

Which resistor in this circuit is considered as the weakest link? Explain.

(2)   Plot the I-V characteristics of R_1, R_2, R_3 and R_T on Graph 3.1.

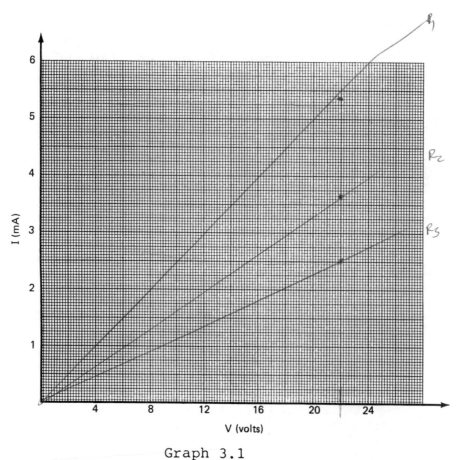

Graph 3.1

(3) What are the effects with respect to the
     voltage across, current through and power
     dissipation of each resistor, if the
     resistance of R_3 is increased? Record your
     answers in Table 3.1 using the following
     simple conventions:

     'increase'   ↑

     'decrease'   ↓

     'no change'   =

Table 3.1

COMPONENT	R	V	I	P
R_1	=	=	=	=
R_2	=	=	=	=
R_3	↑	=	↓	↓
TOTAL	↑	=	↓	↓

Prelab Work Space:

$$P = \frac{V^2}{R} \qquad V = \sqrt{PR}$$

$R_1 = 4.7 k\omega \quad P = \frac{1}{8}w$

$R_2 = 6.8 k\omega \quad P = \frac{1}{2}w$

$R_3 = 10 k\omega \quad P = \frac{1}{2}w$

$V_1 = 48.47 v$

$V_2 = 58.309$

$V_3 = 70.7100$

Max ~~Allowed~~ Voltage

$R_T = 2174.79 \Omega$

$V_T = 48.47$

$I = \frac{V}{R}$

$= \dfrac{48.87}{2174.79}$

$= 22.28 mA$

Prelab Work Space:

$$R_e = \frac{1}{R_T} = \frac{1}{R_1} + \frac{1}{R_2} + \frac{1}{R_3}$$

$$V = I_R$$

$$I = \frac{V}{R}$$

$$\frac{1}{R_T} = \frac{1}{6.8k} + \frac{1}{4.7k} + \frac{1}{10k}$$

$$R_T = 2174.79\,\Omega$$

$$G_e = \frac{1}{R_T} = 4.6 \times 10^{-4}\,S$$

$$I_T = \frac{V_T}{R_1} + \frac{U_T}{R_2} + \frac{U_T}{R_3}$$

$$\frac{I_1}{I_T} = 0.4626 \quad \frac{G_1}{G_T} = 4.08785$$

$$= 5.32mA + 3.68mA + 2.5mA$$

$$= 0.0115A$$

$$\frac{I_2}{I_3} = 0.6917 \quad \frac{G_2}{G_3} = 1.44$$

$$= 11.5\,mA$$

$$P_T = I_T^2 R_T$$

$$P_1 = I_1^2 R_1$$

$$P_2 = I_2^2 R_2$$

$$= (11.5)^2 (2174.79)$$

$$= (5.32mA)^2 (4.7k)$$

$$= (3.68mA)^2 (6.8k)$$

$$= 0.28876W$$

$$= 0.133W$$

$$= 0.092W$$

$$P_3 = I_3^2 R_3$$

$$= (2.5mA)^2 (10k\Omega)$$

$$= 0.0625W$$

$$P_T = I_T^2 R_T$$

$$P = \frac{U^2}{R}$$

$$0.5W = (I_T)^2 (2174.79)$$

$$I_T = 0.01516$$

$$= 15.16\,mA \ \ MAX.$$

1st resistor is the weakest link, current flows first through the resistor

3.3   Equipment:

ITEM	MANUFACTURER AND MODEL NO.	LAB. SERIAL NO
DC Power Supply		
VOM		
DMM or DC milliammeter		

Resistors: One 4.7 kΩ , 6.8 kΩ , 10 kΩ , 15kΩ

3.4   Procedure:

(1)   Connect the circuit shown in Fig 3.2.

The terminal voltage of the power supply is to be set at 25V while the circuit is connected.

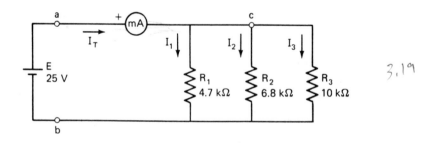

3.19

Fig. 3.2

(2)   Measure the total current supplied from source (I_T). Using the VOM or DMM, check and verify that the voltage across each resistor is 25V. Record your results in Table 3.2.

34

(3) Disconnect the milliammeter from its present location. Measure I_1, I_2, I_3 by connecting the milliammeter in series with the corresponding resistance. Record your results in Table 3.2.

Table 3.2

Component	VOLTMETER		MILLIAMMETER		G (calculated) $= (\dfrac{mA}{volts}) = mS$	Power (calculated) mW $P = U \cdot I$
	Range	Reading (Volts)	Range	Reading (mA)		
DC POWER SUPPLY		25		11.49 mA	$G_T = 0.461\,ms$	286.101 mW
— R_1	200	24.9	20	5.34 mA	$G_1 = 0.214\,ms$	132.966 mW
R_2	200	24.9	20	3.67 mA	$G_2 = 0.147\,ms$	91.383 mW
R_3	200	24.9	20	2.5 mA	$G_3 = 0.100\,ms$	62.25 mW

(4) Calculate the values of G_T, G_1, G_2 and G_3 and the power in each resistor from the current and voltage measurements. Record these values in Table 3.2. Plot the I-V characteristics of R_T using the experimental results, on Graph 3.1.

$$P = \frac{U^2}{R} = R \cdot I^2$$

$$P = U \cdot I$$

(5) Compare the following quantities in Table 3.3 using the experimental results:

Table 3.3

$I_1 + I_2 + I_3 =$ 11.51 mA	$I_T =$ 11.49 mA
$G_1 + G_2 + G_3 =$ -0.461 mS	$G_T =$ 0.461 mS
$\dfrac{I_1}{I_2} =$ 1.45	$\dfrac{G_1}{G_2} =$ 1.45
$\dfrac{I_3}{I_T} =$ 0.217	$\dfrac{G_3}{G_T} =$ 0.217

(6) Replace R_3 in Fig. 3.2 by a 15 kΩ resistor. Measure I_T, I_1, I_2, I_3 and E and record these results in Table 3.4. Calculate the power dissipated in each resistor and the total power.

Table 3.4

E (V)	I_T (mA)	I_1 (mA)	I_2 (mA)	I_3 (mA)	POWER = VI mW			
					P_1	P_2	P_3	P_T
24.9	10.65	5.34	3.67	1.168	132.96	91.38	41.83	230.35

How does the increase in the magnitude of R_3 affect the voltage across, current through and power dissipation of each resistor in the circuit? (Compare the results of Table 3.4 with the results in Table 3.2). Record

these observations in Table 3.1, using the
↑ , ↓ , = convention. [For clarity, use a
different color pencil or pen to emphasize
these observations].

3.5   **Comments and Conclusions:**

1.   Summarize the properties of a DC parallel
circuit. Are these properties supported
by your experimental results? Use the
various data obtained in the experiments
to justify the statements.

— in a parallel circuit, if a path is open circuited,
then it does not affect any other path.
— The total current is equal to the sum of all
the currents in a circuit.
— The electric potential is constant throughout the
entire circuit.
— the total resistance is calculated by

$$\frac{1}{R_T} = \frac{1}{R_1} + \frac{1}{R_2} \cdots \frac{1}{R_n}$$

2. What are the possible causes for any deviations in the experimental results from the theoretical or nominal values?

Deviations include an increase of resistance due to the wires in the circuit.

Also, the % tolerance of each resistor.

3. What are the effects on I_T, I_1, I_2 and I_3 if R_2, for some reason, is:

    (a) open-circuited;

I_T will decrease

I_1, I_3 will remain same

$I_2 = 0$

    (b) short-circuited?

I_T = increase

I_1, I_2, I_3 same

4. Write Kirchhoff's current law at node 'c' in Fig. 3.2.

4 | SERIES-PARALLEL DC CIRCUIT

Required Reading: Text, sections 3.4.2 and 3.6

4.1   Objective:

- To verify Kirchhoff's voltage and current laws in series-parallel circuits.

- To become familiar with the concept of circuit 'ground'.

4.2   Prelab Assignment:

(1)   Consider the circuit shown in Fig. 4.1. The terminal voltage of the power supply is maintained at 25V.

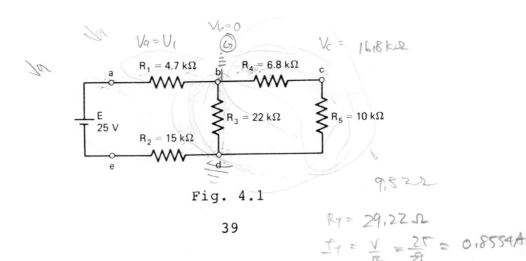

Fig. 4.1

39

(2) Calculate the equivalent resistance of the circuit, voltage drops across and currents through all of the resistors. Record these values under Calculated (CALC) values in Table 4.2.

(3) Calculate the potentials V_a, V_b, V_c, V_d and V_e, assuming:

(a) node 'b' is selected as circuit 'ground',

(b) node 'd' is selected as circuit 'ground'.

Record these values in Table (4.5).

(4) Identify the resistor that would be damaged first as the applied emf is gradually increased, assuming that each resistor is rated 1/2 watt.

(5) Determine the effects with respect to voltage across, current through and power dissipation of each resistor in the circuit, if the resistance of:

(a) R_3 is decreased,

(b) R_1 is increased.

Tabulate your answers in Table 4.1 using ' ↑ , ↓ , = ' convention;

$$P = I^2 R$$
$$I = \sqrt{\frac{P}{R}}$$

$$I_1 = \sqrt{\frac{0.5}{4.7k}} \qquad I_2 = \sqrt{\frac{0.5}{15k}} \qquad I_3 = \sqrt{\frac{0.5}{22k}} \qquad I_4 = \sqrt{\frac{0.5}{6.8k}} \qquad I_5 = \sqrt{\frac{0.5}{10k}}$$

$$0.01 \qquad 5.77mA \qquad 4.76mA \qquad 8.57mA \qquad 7.07mA$$

Table 4.1

(a) R_3: decreased

COMPONENT	R	V	I	P
R_1	=	↑	↑	↑
R_2	=	↑	↑	↑
R_3	↓	↓	↑	↑
R_4	=	↓	↓	↓
R_5	=	↓	↑	↓
TOTAL	↓	=	↑	↑

$V = I \cdot R$

Table 4.1

(b) R_1: increased

COMPONENT	R	V	I	P
R_1	↑	↑	↓	↓
R_2	=	↓	↓	↓
R_3	=	↑	↓	↓
R_4	=	↓	↓	↓
R_5	=	↓	↓	↓
TOTAL	↑	=	↓	↓

Prelab Work Space:

4.3   <u>Equipment:</u>

ITEM	MANUFACTURER AND MODEL NO.	LAB. SERIAL NO
DC Power Supply		
VOM		
DMM or DC milliammeter		
Decade Resistance Box		

<u>Resistors:</u> One 4.7 kΩ , 6.8 kΩ , 10 kΩ , 15kΩ

and 22 kΩ .

4.4   **Procedure:**

A.   <u>Verification of KVL and KCL:</u>

(1)   Connect the circuit as shown in Fig. 4.2.   Set the
output voltage of the power supply at 25V while the
circuit is connected.

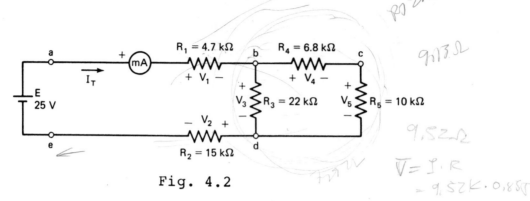

Fig. 4.2

(2)   Measure the total current (I_T) supplied
from the source; the voltage drops
V_1, V_2, V_3, V_4, V_5 and the applied
voltage E.   Record your results in
Table 4.2.

(3)   Disconnect the ammeter from its present
location and reconnect it back in the
circuit at various locations in order to
measure I_2, I_3, I_4 and I_5 successively.
Record these results in Table 4.2.

Table 4.2

$V = I \cdot R$

		E (V)	V_1 (V)	V_2 (V)	V_3 (V)	V_4 (V)	V_5 (V)
VOLTS	CALC (V) -Prelab	25	4.01	12.8	8.13	3.287 =9.52Ω	4.89
	EXPT. (V)	25	4.02	12.8	8.15	3.29	4.85
		I_T	I_1	I_2	I_3	I_4	I_5
CURRENTS	CALC. (mA) -Prelab	0.855	0.855	0.855	0.369	0.9639	0.2984
	EXPT. (mA)	0.853		0.854	.372	0.481	0.480
		R_T	R_1	R_2	R_3	R_4	R_5
RESISTANCE	-Prelab (kΩ)	29.22	4.7	15	22	6.8	10
	EXPT. (kΩ)	29	4.7	19.8	21.9	6.8	10

(4) Replace R_3 in the circuit of Fig. 4.2 by a decade resistance box. Set the resistance of the box at 5 kΩ . Measure E, I_T, V_1, V_2, V_3, V_4, V_5, I_1, I_2, I_3, I_4 and I_5. Record these results in Table 4.3.

1/1

1/10

1/100

5

Table 4.3

$R_3 = 5\ k\Omega$

4,7   15   5k   6,8   10

E (V)	V_1 (V)	V_2 (V)	V_3 (V)	V_4 (V)	V_5 (V)	I_T (mA)	I_1 (mA)	I_2 (mA)	I_3 (mA)	I_4 (mA)	I_5 (mA)
25	5,01	15,95	4,09	1,65	2,43	1,059	1,06	1,06	0,810	0,241	0,240

(5) Return R_3 back to the circuit
(R_3 = 22 kΩ) and now replace R_1 by a
decade resistance box set to 25 kΩ .
Measure all the voltages and currents in
the circuit. Record the results in
Table 4.4.

Table 4.4

$R_1 = 25\ k\Omega$

E (V)	V_1 (V)	V_2 (V)	V_3 (V)	V_4 (V)	V_5 (V)	I_T (mA)	I_1 (mA)	I_2 (mA)	I_3 (mA)	I_4 (mA)	I_5 (mA)
25	7,96	12,61	8,48	3,43	5,05	0,838	0,839	0,838	0,339	0,499	0,499

(6) Compare the results in Tables 4.3 and
4.4 with the corresponding quantities
in Table 4.2 and superimpose the
observations in Table 4.1, using
' ↑ , ↓ , = ' convention.

B.   Concept of circuit 'ground':

(1) With node 'b' as circuit 'ground', measure V_a, V_c, V_d, V_e. [Hint: one terminal of the voltmeter is connected to node 'b'.] Record your results in Table 4.5.

(2) With node 'd' as circuit 'ground' (instead of node 'b'), measure V_a, V_b, V_c, V_e. Record your results in Table 4.5.

Table 4.5

Potential	'b' circuit ground		'd' circuit ground	
	CALC Prelab (V)	EXPT. (V)	CALC Prelab (V)	EXPT. (V)
V_a	4.01	4.03 ~~3.96~~	−12.8	12.22
V_b	0	6	8.13	8.18
V_c	−8.29	−3.31	~~8.13~~ 4.85	4.87
V_d	−8.13	−8.18	0	0
V_e	25	0	−12.8	−12.84

47

4.5   <u>Comments and Conclusions:</u>

1.   Apply Kirchhoff's voltage and current
       laws to the series-parallel circuit in
       Fig. 4.2. Were these laws supported by
       your experimental results? Explain.

Yes, The two fundamental laws were
supported by the experiment. First,
The sum of the voltage Drops in any
closed loop added up to the applied
secondly, the current entering into
any node was equal to the current
exiting the node. The experiment
proves that in KVL & KCL work in
series - parallel circuits

2. What are the possible causes for any deviations in the experimental results from the theoretical values?

All equipment, including wire resistor and meters all have small internal resistance which affect the outcome of the experiments. Also, the resistor may not be exactly the specified value. They could have a slight deviations of about ± 50% tolerance

3. What is a circuit 'ground' and why is there a necessity of a circuit 'ground' in some circuits? A circuit ground is a point of reference. Some circuits require both a +ve and +ve points for reference. A ground allows us to accomplish this task

4. Explain the effects of moving the circuit ground from 'b' to 'd' on:

(a) currents in the circuit,

Moving ground in the circuit from B to D will have absolutely No effect on the current or the circuit

(b)   voltage drops across the resistors,

changing the ground from B to D did not change the voltage. Drop across the resistors in the circuit.

(c)   potentials of various nodes.

V_a – increases
V_b – increases
V_c – increase
V_d increases
V_e – increased

5.   During experimentation with the node 'b' as circuit ground, node 'd' was accidentally grounded. What are the effects on currents and voltages in the circuit due to such an incident? Draw the equivalent circuit of Fig. 4.2 for this condition.

If D was accidentally grounded, the total resistance of the circuit would decrease and current increase V_1 & V_2 would also increase

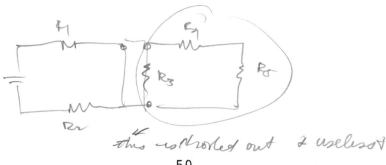

this is crossed out & useless

5 | WHEATSTONE BRIDGE

5 MAX marks.

<u>Required Reading:</u>   Text, section 3.7

5.1   **Objective:**

To understand the principle and performance of the Wheatstone bridge.

5.2   **Prelab Assignment:**

A.   <u>Simple Methods of Measuring Unknown Resistance:</u>

Explain the procedure with the necessary circuit diagrams that can be used in the laboratory to measure an unknown resistance given the following sets of equipment only.

(1)   <u>Set # 1:</u>

one DC power supply

one voltmeter

one ammeter

51

(2)   Set # 2:

one DC power supply

one voltmeter

one decade resistance box

Explain the limitations of each of the above methods.

B.   Wheatstone bridge:

The circuit of Fig. 5.1 shows a simple schematic of the Wheatstone bridge. R_1 and R_2 can each have three possible settings: $10\,\Omega$, $100\,\Omega$ and $1000\,\Omega$. R_3 is a decade resistance box with a maximum possible value of $9999\,\Omega$. R_X is the unknown resistor and may assume any value from $1\,m\Omega$ to a high value of $1\,M\Omega$.

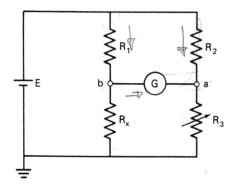

Fig. 5.1

1(a)   Determine the values of R_1, R_2, R_3 and R_X which result in the potentials V_a to be as large as possible and V_b to be as small as possible. What is the direction

52

of the current flow through the
galvanometer (G): from 'a' towards 'b'
or 'b' to 'a'?

(b)   If the unknown resistor R_x is variable
and is gradually increased, how would
this change affect the magnitudes of
V_a and V_b? Determine the value of
R_x (max) at which V_a and V_b are equal
with the settings of R_1, R_2 and R_3
as in (a).

$$\frac{R_1}{R_x} = \frac{R_2}{R_3}$$

$$\frac{10}{R_0} = 10$$

(c)   If R_x is larger than R_x (max), what
would be the direction of current flow
through the galvanometer? Could the
bridge be balanced under this condition
with the settings of R_1, R_2 and R_3
available on the bridge? Explain.

(2)   Suppose that an unknown resistance (R_x)
is in the range of 0 to 99 Ω and is to
be measured using the above bridge. What
are the best settings of R_1 and R_2 that
can achieve the optimum accuracy of a
measurement of R_x? [Note: R_3 has a
maximum value consisting of four digits.]

1. ref: The ammeter is used to measure
   the current flowing through the
   bridge. If the bridge is (00)
   the then resistors are balanced
   The same could be used for a
   voltmeter.

q) I $a \sim b$

$$\frac{R1}{Rx} = \frac{R2}{R3} \qquad \frac{1000}{Rx} = \frac{10}{9999}$$

$$Rx = 9999 \, \Omega$$

limitations: R is unknown
no odea of current supply
will damage circuit

Rint is unknown so
current is also unknown.
may damage system.

1 a) $\frac{R1}{Rx} = \frac{R2}{R3}$ $\frac{100}{Rx} = \frac{10}{999}$ $\frac{1000}{Rx} = \frac{10}{999}$ $\frac{10}{Rx} = \frac{1000}{9999}$

$\frac{10}{Rx} = \frac{10}{9999}$ $Rx = 99990$ $Rx = 999900$ Rx 99.99

$Rx = 9999$

5.3   Equipment:

ITEM	MANUFACTURER AND MODEL NO.	LAB. SERIAL NO
DC Power Supply		
VOM		
DMM or DC milliammeter		
Commercial Wheatstone Bridge		
Decade Resistance Boxes: Three Nos.		
Galvanometer or Null Detector		

Resistors: One 47 Ω , 470 Ω , 6.8 kΩ

5.4   Procedure:

A.   Simple Methods:

1(a) Assume that 470 Ω resistor is the unknown resistance (R_x). Using the equipment of Set #1 (Prelab), measure the unknown resistance. Set the output voltage of DC power supply at 10V. Read the milliammeter and voltmeter readings as accurately as possible. Record the results in Table 5.1.

1(b) Repeat step (a) with R_x = 6.8 k Ω . Record the results in Table 5.1.

Table 5.1

R (nominal)	Voltmeter reading (V)	Ammeter reading (mA)	R_x (calculated)
470 Ω	10.03	21.3	470.89 Ω ~~483.56 Ω~~
6.8 kΩ	10.03	1.46	6.869 kΩ

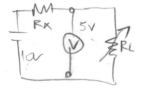

(2) Use the **equipment** of Set # 2 (Prelab).
With the DC power supply set at 10V,
measure the unknown resistance,
assuming 470 Ω and 6.8 kΩ resistors
as unknown values. Record the values in
Table 5.2.

Table 5.2

R (nominal)	R (Decade box)	R_x
470 Ω	4.7 ~~0100 kΩ 6.8~~	~~470~~
6.8 kΩ	~~1000~~K 6.8	6800

B.   Wheatstone bridge:

(1) Connect the circuit of Fig. 5.2.

set E = 5V

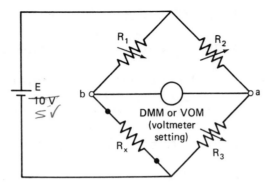

Fig. 5.2

Set E = $\overset{5\checkmark}{\cancel{10}}$V, R_3 at its <u>maximum</u> value and

R_x = 470 Ω. Set the VOM at a higher

voltage scale. Select the values of

R_1 = 100 Ω and R_2 = 1000 Ω.

Balance the bridge by reducing R_3 till

the voltage V_{ab} is zero or as close to

zero as possible. Accurate balance of

the bridge can be achieved by reducing

the voltage scales of VOM and adjusting

R_3 further till the voltmeter reads zero.

Record the value of R_3 and calculate

R_x.

(2) Repeat the measurements for the various

values of R_1, R_2 and R_x shown in

Table 5.3. <u>Before each new setting of</u>

<u>R_1 and R_2 are selected, R_3 should be</u>

<u>adjusted back to its maximum value and</u>

<u>the VOM on a higher scale.</u>

<u>Caution:</u> If the VOM is used in the current mode

(a current detector) or a galvanometer is used

(instead of VOM) between the points a-b, it is

advisable to use a potentiometer or a variable

57

resistance in series with the instrument to protect it. Resistance is set at its highest value initially. As the bridge is brought closer and closer to the balanced condition, this resistance can be reduced to obtain a better sensitivity of the detector.

Table 5.3

	R_x (nominal)	R_1 (Ω)	R_2 (Ω)	R_3 (Ω)	$R_x = (\frac{R_1}{R_2})\, R_3$
		100	1000	4500	450Ω
(a)	470 Ω	100	100	460	460
		1000	100	47	470
		100	1000	68000	6800
(b)	6800 Ω	100	100	6800	6800
		1000	100	684	6840
		100	1000	480	48
(c)	47 Ω	100	100	49	49
		1000	100	5	50

C.   Commercial Wheatstone bridge:

In commercial bridges, R_1 and R_2 are variable in decades so that the ratio of R_1/R_2 is an integral multiplier or decimal

58

and is normally called 'multiplier ratio' or 'ratio arm'. R_3 is a decade resistor (or a slide wire rheostat). Null detector is usually a sensitive galvanometer with a push-button switch and a potentiometer in series with the detector.

(1) Record all the ratios of (R_1/R_2) available on the bridge and also the maximum-value of R_3 obtainable. This data would enable you to decide on which of the ratios of (R_1/R_2) are useful in measuring R_x.

(2) With R_x set at $470 \, \Omega$, measure the value of R_x for all the possible ratios of (R_1/R_2). Record the results in Table 5.4.

(3) Repeat (2) for $R_x = 6800 \, \Omega$ and $R_x = 47 \, \Omega$. Record the results in Table 5.4.

Table 5.4

	R_x (nominal)	(R_1/R_2)	R_3	$R_x = (\frac{R_1}{R_2})\, R_3$	% Error
(a)	470 Ω				
(b)	6800 Ω				
(c)	47 Ω				

$$\% \text{ Error} = \frac{[R_x(\text{measured}) - R_x(\text{nominal})]}{R_x(\text{nominal})} \times 100$$

5.5 Comments and Conclusions:

1. What are the various methods used in the laboratory for measuring unknown resistance?

1. Using a Decade box of known value & vom to the determine voltage drops.

2. Using a voltmeter and power supply and ohmeter

3. Wheatstone bridge.

2. Which of the methods in (1) is the most accurate one? Explain.

Based on the results the Decade Box was the most accurate. It may seem odd however, the values depend on the accuracy of the equipment.

3. What are the limitations in measuring R_X using methods in Part (A)?

The methods in part A require the equipment to be accurate any Deviations could cause slight errors.

4. What are the maximum and minimum values of R_X that can be measured in:

(a) circuit of Fig. 5.2,

If $R_1 = 100$ and 1000 $R_2 = 100$ and 1000

R_X can be measured from $R_3 \times 10$ max

to R_3 MIN $\div 10$.

(b) commercial Wheatstone bridge?

5. How can the Wheatstone bridge be used as a:

(a) Thermometer,

R_X could be a temperature sensitive resistor. Which changes in temperature. The resistance of R_X would change proportionally. This change can be used to measure change in temperature

(b) Lie-detector?

The body could be hooked up in R_X position. When the body tells a lie, the resistance will change causing the bridge to become unbalanced. The VOM will read a different value

6 | PRACTICAL DC SOURCES

Required Reading: Text, section 4.1 to 4.5

6.1   Objective:

- To find the parameters of a practical DC source and investigate the behaviour of a practical DC source under varying load conditions.

- To become familiar with the 'load line' concept.

- To understand the 'maximum power transfer' principle.

6.2   Prelab Assignment:

Consider a DC power supply with the following characteristics:

-terminal voltage is 35V on no-load condition and 30 volts when a load of $270\,\Omega$ is connected to the terminals:

-internal resistance is unknown.

(1) Calculate the internal resistance of the source.

(2) Plot the load line (regulation curve) of the power supply on Graph 6.1. Draw the V-I characteristic of the 270 Ω load on the same graph. Determine graphically the load current (I_L) and voltage (V_L) across the load.

(3) A variable resistance load (R_L) is connected across the power supply and varied over a range of 5 to 500 Ω in the steps shown in Table 6.1. Calculate the values of I_L, V_L, P_L, the total power supplied from the source and the efficiency of the power transfer for each setting of R_L. Record these results in Table 6.1.

Table 6.1

$V_L = 30v$

R_L (Ω) $\frac{E}{R_{INT}+R_L}$	5	20	40	45	50	60	100	200	500
I_L (mA)	700	538	412	389	368	333	241	143	65
V_L (V)	3.5	10.76	16.48	17.5	18.4	19.98	24.1	28.6	32
P_L (W)	2.45	5.78	6.79	6.6	6.77	6.65	5.8	4.04	2.05
P_T (W) $I_L^2 R_T$	24.5	18.8	19.4	13.61	12.88	11.7	8.4	5.0	2.29
% Efficiency $=(P_L/P_T) \times 100$	10%	31%	47%	50%	52%	57%	69%	81%	92%

64

(4) Plot the graphs of the load current (I_L) versus R_L and the voltage across the load (V_L) versus R_L on Graph 6.2.

(5) Plot the graphs of the power dissipated in the load (P_L) and the power-transfer efficiency versus the load resistance (R_L) on Graph 6.3.

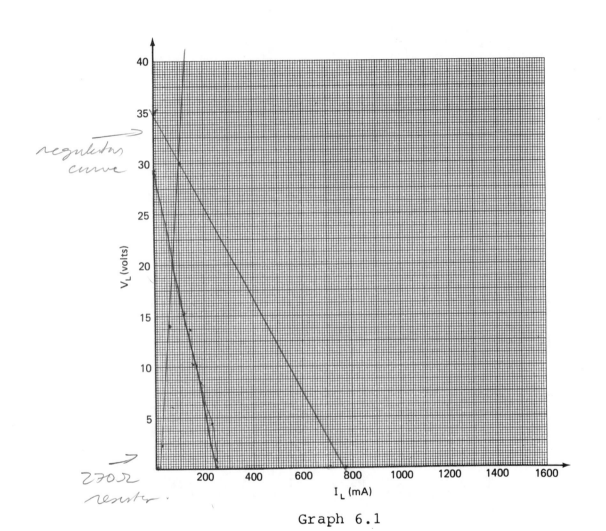

Graph 6.1

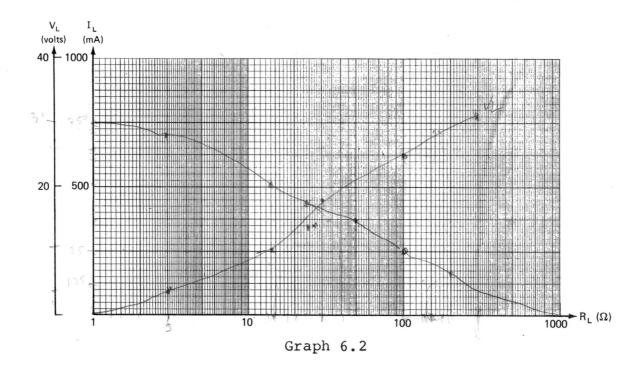

Graph 6.2

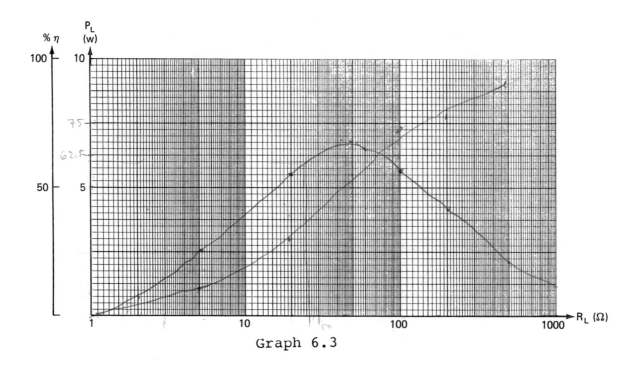

Graph 6.3

66

Prelab Work Space:

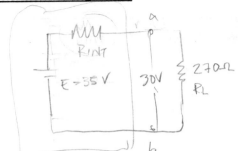

$V_{IN} : E = R_{INT} I$

$$\frac{35}{R_{INT}} = I$$

$V = E - R_{INT} I$

$30 = 35 - R_{INT} \left(\frac{5}{9}\right)$

$-5 = \frac{-R_{INT} I}{9}$

$R_{INT} = \boxed{45 \,\Omega}$

$V_C = 30$

$R_L = 270$

$35-30$

$35 = 30 + U$

$V = 5$ voltage drop.

$I_{sc} = \frac{V}{R_{INT}} = \frac{35}{45} = 0.77$

$I = \frac{U_L}{R_L} = \frac{30}{270}$

$= \frac{1}{9}$ A

② i) $R_7 = 50\Omega$

$I_L = \frac{35}{50} = 0.70 A$

$U_C = 0.7 \times 5 = 3.5 V$

$P_L = 3.5 \times 0.7 = 2.45 W$

ii) $R_7 = 65\Omega$

$I_L = \frac{35}{65} = 0.5385 A$

$V_C = 0.5385 \times 120 = 10.769 V$

$P_L = 0.5385 \times 10.769 = 5.8 W$

iii) $R_7 = 85\Omega$

$I_L = \frac{35}{85} = 0.41176 A$

$U_C = 0.411 \times 40 = 16.471 U$

$P_L = 0.411 \times 16.47 = 6.98 W$

iv) $R_7 = 90\Omega$

$I_L = \frac{35}{90} = 0.3889 A$

$V_C = 0.388 \times 45 = 17.5 U$

$P_L = 0.3899 \times 17.5 = 6.806 W$

v) $R_7 = 95$

$I_L = 0.3689 A$

$V_C = 18.92 V$

$P_L = 6.786 W$

vi) $R_7 = 105\Omega$

$I_L = 0.33 A$

$V_C = 20 V.$

$P_L = 6.67 W$

vii) $R_7 = 145\Omega$

$I_L = 0.2419$

$V_C = 24.14 V$

$P_L = 5.827.$

viii) $R_7 = 245\Omega$

$I_L = 0.143 A$

$V_L = 28.57 V$

$P_L = 4.086 W$

ix) $R_7 = 545\Omega$

$I_L = 0.64 A$

$U_L = 32 U$

$P_L = 32 \times 0.64 = 2.45 W.$

Equipment:

ITEM	MANUFACTURER AND MODEL NO.	LAB. SERIAL NO
DC Power Supply		
VOM		
DMM or DC milliammeter		
Decade Resistance Box		

Resistors: One 47 Ω .

6.4   **Procedure:**

(1)   Connect the circuit as shown in Fig. 6.1.
Set the no-load or open-circuit voltage (E)
of the power supply at 30V (without R_L).
Consider R_1 as though it is part of the
internal resistance.

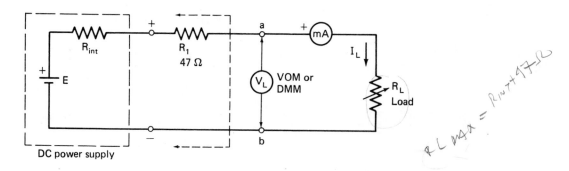

Fig. 6.1

68

(2) Vary the load resistor by the values shown in Table 6.2 and for each setting, measure the current through the load (I_L) and the voltage across the load (V_L). Record the results in Table 6.2. Calculate P_L, P_T and efficiency of the power transfer for each value of R_L and record these values in Table 6.2.

Table 6.2

R_L (Ω)	5	20	40	45	50	60	80	100	200	500
I_L (mA)									14.7	5.9
V_L (V)									28.2	29.3
P_L (W)										
P_T (W)										
% Efficiency = (P_L/P_T) x 100										

(3) Superimpose the V_L versus I_L graph on Graph 6.1. From the measured data, determine the actual internal resistance (R_{int}) of the power supply. $R_{int} = $ slope of graph. $\dfrac{\Delta v}{\Delta I} = \dfrac{19 - 1.3}{0.14 - 0.297} = \dfrac{12.7}{0.107} = \simeq 116\Omega$

(4) Estimate the short-circuit current (I_{sc}) from the above graph.

69

(5) Plot the V-I characteristic of R_L = 50Ω on Graph 6.1 and determine graphically the voltage across and current through R_L. Compare this value with the measured value in Table 6.2.

$$\frac{9.1}{0.181} = 50.27 \text{ Ω}$$

(6) Superimpose the graphs of I_L versus R_L and V_L versus R_L on Graph 6.2; the graphs of P_L and efficiency versus R_L on Graph 6.3.

6.5 Comments and Conclusions:

1. What should be the value of the internal resistance relative to the load resistance of a good voltage source? Relatively large or relatively small. Explain.

    small because we want the lowest potential drop as possible

2. What should be the value of the internal resistance relative to R_L of a good current source? Relatively large or relatively small. Explain.

    As large as possible because we don't want a current flow

3. For what value of R_L, is maximum power transferred to the load?

    Load R= equall to total resistor

4. What is the value of the power transfer efficiency at the maximum power transfer condition?

    50%

    $$P_L = \frac{E^2}{4 \, RINT}$$

5. Do you consider the 'DC power supply' used in this experiment a good voltage source? Explain.

    poor regulation
    output terminal an power supply drop

6. If the load is a non-linear resistor whose
    V-I characteristic is given, explain how you
    would determine the current and voltage across
    the load when connected to the above DC supply.

Take multiple points draw the best fit line
then where it intersects is the
    I & V across the load

7. Compare and comment on the experiment results
    with respect to the expected prelab results.
    Explain the reasons for deviations.

We used a different voltage
and different value for the
resistance

7 | VOLTAGE DIVIDERS

Required Reading: Text, section 4.6

7.1   Objective:

To become familiar with 'voltage divider' concepts.

7.2   Prelab Assignment:

A.   Divider for a Variable Load:

Design a voltage divider to supply power to a varying load, using a DC power supply with an open-circuit voltage of 25V and an internal resistance of 45 Ω . The load voltage (V_L) must remain within the range of $10V \leq V_L \leq 11$ volts, while the load (R_L) is allowed to vary over the range $1 \text{ k}\Omega \leq R_L \leq 10 \text{ k}\Omega$.

B. _Divider for Multiple Loads:_

Design a voltage divider to supply the
following loads:

3 mA at + 14   volts,

1 mA at - 10 volts.

The source has an open-circuit voltage of 30V
and an internal resistance of 45 Ω .   The
supply current is limited to 10 mA.

Prelab Work Space:

$$I_4 = \frac{10v}{1k\Omega} = 0.01A$$

$$I_{L2} = \frac{11v}{10k\Omega} = 0.0011A$$

$$\Delta R = \frac{\Delta V}{\Delta I} = \frac{11-10}{0.0011 - 0.01} = -112.9$$

$$V = RI = V_{oc}$$

$$10 = -112.36(0.01) + V_{oc}$$

$$V_{oc} = 11.124V$$

$$0 = -112.36(I_{sc}) + 11.29$$

$$I_{sc} = \frac{-11.129}{-112.36}$$

$$= 0.099A$$

$$SC. \quad V_{RINT} = I_{sc} R_{INT}$$

$$= 0.099(45)$$

$$= 4.46V$$

74

Prelab Work Space:

$V_{RSP} = 25 - 4.46 = 20.54 V$

$$\frac{V_{RB}}{V_T} = \frac{R_B}{R_T} \qquad R_{SD} = \frac{V_{RSD}}{I_{SC}} = \frac{20.54}{0.099} = 207.5 \, \Omega$$

$$\frac{11.129}{25} = \frac{R_b}{45\Omega + 207.5 + R_B}$$

$$25 R_B = 11.129 R_B + 2806.81$$

$$R_B = 202.4 \, \Omega$$

(B)

$\mathcal{E}_{max} = 30 V \qquad V_{int} = (45)(10mA) \qquad R_1 = \frac{14}{7mA} = 2000\Omega$

$I_{max} = 10mA \qquad \qquad = 0.45 V \qquad \qquad R_2 = \frac{10}{9mA} = 1111\Omega$

$V_{RSD} = \mathcal{E} - V_{RINT} - U_S$

$\quad = 30 - 0.45 - 24$

$\quad = 5.55 V$

$R_{SD} = \frac{5.55 V}{10mA} = 555 \, \Omega$

75

Prelab Work Space:

ITEM	MANUFACTURER AND MODEL NO.	LAB. SERIAL NO
DC Power Supply		
VOM		
DMM or DC milliammeter		
Decade Resistance Box: 3 Nos.		

Resistors: One 4.7 kΩ and 10 kΩ .

7.4   **Procedure:**

A: **Divider for a Variable Load:**

(1) Connect the circuit as in Fig. 7.1 using
your design of the voltage divider. Adjust
the open-circuit voltage of a DC power supply
to 25V. Use the three decade resistance
boxes to represent the voltage divider and
the variable load (R_L).

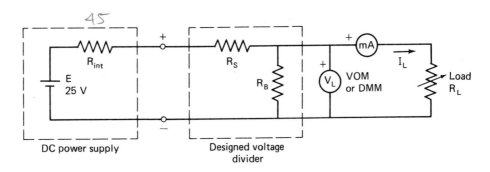

Fig. 7.1

The Voltage divider has a series-drop resistor (R_S) and a bleeder resistor (R_B). [If the internal resistance of the power supply is different from 45 Ω , adjust the series-drop resistor to account for the change in the internal resistance.]

(2) Set the values of R_L to the various values as suggested in Table 7.1 and measure I_L and V_L for each of these values. Record these results in the table.

Table 7.1

R_L (kΩ)	10	9	7	5	4	3	2	1
I_L (mA)	1,053	1,178	1,317	2,13	2,63	3,29	5,12	
V_L (V)	10,68	10,67	10,64	10,64	10,56	10,46	10.29	9,74

(3) Plot the voltage regulation characteristics on Graph 7.1.

78

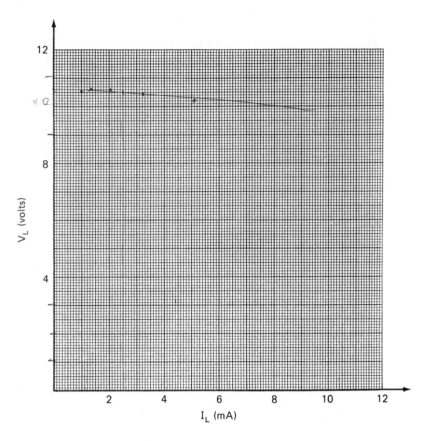

Graph 7.1

B. Divider for Multiple Loads:

(1) Connect the circuit as in Fig. 7.2 using
     your design of the voltage divider. Set the
     open-circuit voltage of a DC power supply to
     30 volts. Use the three decade resistance
     boxes to represent the designed voltage
     divider. [If the internal resistance of the
     power supply is different from 45 Ω , the
     series-drop resistor must be adjusted
     correspondingly.]

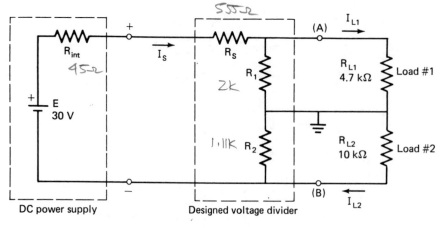

Fig. 7.2

(2) Use the milliammeter or DMM in the ammeter mode to measure the current supplied from the source (I_S) and the load currents I_{L1} and I_{L2}. Measure the potential V_A and V_B. Record your results in Table 7.2.

Table 7.2

V_A (V)	I_{L1} (mA)	P_{L1} (mW)	V_B (V)	I_{L2} (mA)	P_{L2} (mW)	I_S (mA)	P_T (mW)
13.9v	2.95	41	-9.8	0.99	9.7	9.83	295

(3) Calculate the efficiency of the power transfer from the source to the loads:

$$\% \text{ Efficiency} = \frac{(P_{L1} + P_{L2})}{P_T} \times 100$$

7.5   **Comments and Conclusions:**

1. What are the advantages and disadvantages of a simple voltage divider with the bleeder resistor compared with the divider without the bleeder?

   advantages - allows to reduce the amount of voltage regulation of the divider. It can maintain at nearly fixed voltages.

   disadvant. - cost of same supplyers always require a fluctuation in voltage

2. Consider the voltage divider of Part A; Calculate:

   (a) Ratio of I_B/I_L at loads 1 kΩ and 10 kΩ ,

   (b) I_B as a percentage of the total current supplied from the source at the above loads.

   Comment on the advantage and disadvantage of the voltage divider, based on the data you calculated in (a) and (b).

   a) $I_b = 1k\Omega = 49.5 mA \rightarrow$ 10kΩ $I_b = 53.5 mA$
   $I_c = 1k\Omega = 10 mA \rightarrow$ $I_c = 1.08 mA$

   Various loads can be supplied by one source only. The main problem is it difficult to keep voltage constant. also draws inefficient power dissipation

3. How can the voltage regulation of the divider with the bleeder be improved? What compromise is necessary to improve the regulation as you suggested?

By decreasing the size of R_{B1} the regulation of the divider is improved. When sacrifice is a lower efficiency of the load in the circuit.

4. What is the effect on the current through and voltage drop across R_2, if R_1 in the voltage divider of Fig. 7.2 is shorted-out during the operation of the circuit? Assume that the power supply maintains a constant output voltage.

If R_1 is shorted-out, the current through R_2 will increase and the voltage drop across it will decrease as calculated by ohm's law.

5. Compare and comment on the experimental
results with respect to expected prelab
calculations. Explain the possible reasons
for any deviations.

After modifications of the original pre-lab
assignment the calculated values for Rod
and Rd then agreed with the experimental
values. Equipment, Roundoff errors and
metre sensitivity all allowed for small
errors in the lab.

8 | THEVENIN'S THEOREM

Required Reading: Text, sections 5.1, 5.2, 6.2 and 6.3.

8.1   Objective:

To verify Thevenin's theorem.

8.2   Prelab Assignment:

Consider the circuit shown in Fig. 8.1.

R_L is a variable load with the following resistance settings:

50 Ω , 100 Ω , 1.0 kΩ , 1.25 kΩ , 1.5 kΩ ,

10 kΩ , 20 kΩ and 30 kΩ .

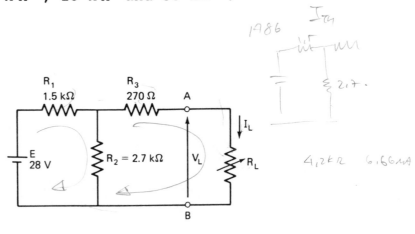

Fig. 8.1

A. Series-Parallel Circuit: Analysis by Loop
    or Mesh-Current Method

    Using the "Loop current" analysis,
determine the values of V_L and I_L for each
setting of R_L. Record these values in
Table 8.2.

B. Thevenin's Theorem:

    (a) Find the Thevenin's equivalent circuit
         parameters as seen at the terminals A-B.
         Record your values in Table 8.1.

    (b) Draw the Thevenin's equivalent circuit
         and using this circuit, calculate the
         voltage (V_L) across and current (I_L)
         through R_L for each setting of R_L.
         Record these values in Table 8.2.

$RL =$

	50	100	1000	1250	1500	10000	20000	30000
$R_T = \dfrac{1}{\frac{1}{RL+270} + \frac{1}{2700}} + 1500$	1786	1825	2363.7	2472.5	2569.12	3637.9	3882.6	3978.8
$I_T = \dfrac{V_T}{R_T} = \dfrac{28}{R_T} =$ mA	15.67	15.34	11.84	11.32	10.9	7.70	7.21	7.03
$\dot{V_1} = R_1 I_T = 1500\,\dot{I}_T$	23.5	23.01	17.76	16.98	16.35	11.55	10.815	10.545
$I_L = \dfrac{V_1}{R_3 + R_L} = \dfrac{V_1}{270 + RL}$ mA	73	62.2	13.98	11.17	9.23	1.12	0.533	0.348
$V_L = I_L \cdot RL$	3.65	6.22	13.98	13.9685	13.845	11.2	10.66	10.49

$$28 = (1500 + 2700\,)I_1$$

$$28 = (1500 + 270 + 50)I_2$$

$$28 = 4200\,I_1$$

$$28 = 1820\,I_2$$

87

Prelab Work Space:

8.3　　　<u>Equipment:</u>

ITEM	MANUFACTURER AND MODEL NO.	LAB. SERIAL NO
DC Power Supply		
VOM		
DMM or DC milliammeter		
Decade Resistance Box		

<u>Resistors:</u>　One 270 Ω , 1.5 kΩ and 2.7 kΩ .

8.4　　　**<u>Procedure:</u>**

A:　<u>Series-Parallel Circuit:</u>

(1)　Connect the circuit as in Fig. 8.2.

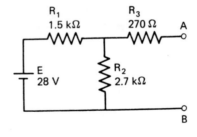

Fig. 8.2

(2)　Connect a decade resistance box (R_L) across the A-B terminals with the necessary instruments to measure I_L and V_L. For each setting of R_L as shown in Table 8.2, measure I_L and V_L and record the results in Table 8.2.

B. Thevenin's Equivalent Circuit:

(1) Remove the load R_L. Measure the open-circuit voltage between the terminals A-B. Record this value of voltage as V_{Th} in Table 8.1.

(2) Connect a milliammeter between the terminals A-B and measure the short-circuit current (I_{AB}); calculate ($R_{Th} = V_{Th}/I_{AB}$). Record this result in Table 8.1.

Table 8.1

	V_{Th} (V)	R_{Th} (Ω)
CALCULATED (Prelab)	18V	1234.28 Ω
EXPERIMENTAL (Measured)	18.1V	$I_{AB}=14.72$ mA 1229.62 Ω

(3) Connect the circuit shown in Fig. 8.3. Set the magnitudes of V_{Th} and R_{Th} to the measured values in Table 8.1.

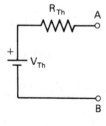

Fig. 8.3

90

Connect the load resistance (R_L) between the
terminals A-B with the necessary instruments to
measure I_L and V_L. For each setting of R_L as
shown in Table 8.2, measure and record the
values of I_L and V_L in the same table.

Table 8.2

R_L (Ω)	PRELAB CALCULATIONS				EXPERIMENTAL RESULTS			
	Loop-Current Analysis		Thevenin's Circuit		Series-Parallel Circuit		Thevenin's Circuit	
	V_L (V)	I_L (mA)	V_L (V)	I_L (mA)	V_L (V)	I_L (mA)	V_L (V)	I_L (mA)
50	0,7	−14mA			0.68	14.13		
100	1.349	−13.49mA			1.32	13.62		
1000	8.05	8.05mA			7.95	8.1		
1250	9.05	7.29mA			8.9	7.28		
1500	9.87	6.58mA			9.72	6.62		
10000	16	1.6 mA			16.	1.62		
20000	16.94	0.847mA			16.9	0.848		
30000	17.28	0.576mA			17.2	0.579		

8.5   Comments and Conclusions:

1. Explain 'Thevenin's Theorem' in words.

The theorem states that a entire network
between two terminals can be replaced
with a simple series circuit with a
voltage source V_{TH} and one resistance
R_{TH}.

2. Draw the 'Norton's equivalent' circuit for the network in Fig. 8.2.

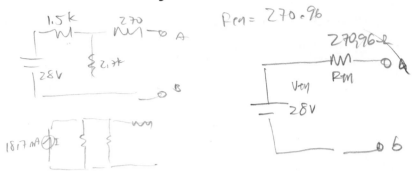

3. For what value of R_L, is maximum power transferred to the load? Calculate the maximum power transferred in the circuit.

when $R_L = R_{TH}$

$$P_{TH} = \frac{V^2}{R_{TH}}$$

$$= \frac{28^2}{220.96}$$

$$= 2.89 W$$

4. Calculate the power dissipated at values of R_L equal to 1 kΩ , 1.25 kΩ and 1.5 kΩ . Are these values less or more than the maximum power? Explain.

270.96

28V

1000Ω
1.25k
1.5k

$I = 22nA$

$$P_1 = I^2 R$$
$$= 0.48 W$$

$$P_2 = (0.0189)^2 (1250)$$
$$= 0.4236 W$$

$$P_3 = (0.0158)^2 (1500)$$
$$= 0.37 W$$

5. Do the experimental results correspond to the theoretical values? If not, explain the reasons for the deviations.

Yes, the results from the calculation do respond with the experimental values.

9 | DC METERS

Required Reading: Text, sections 7.1 to 7.4

9.1   **Objectives:**

(1)   To measure the sensitivity and internal
         resistance of a Metermovement (MM).

(2)   To design, build and calibrate:

(a)   a multi-range voltmeter,

(b)   a milliammeter,

(c)   an ohmmeter.

(3)   To understand the 'loading effects' of the
         meters.

9.2   **Prelab Assignment:**

(1)   Consider a metermovement with a sensitivity
         (S_m) of 2.5 kΩ/volt and an internal
         resistance (R_m) of 500 Ω. Using this
         metermovement, design:

(a) a multi-range voltmeter with 0-10V and 0-25V ranges,

(b) a milliammeter with a range of 0-10 mA,

(c) an ohmmeter with a midscale of 800 Ω using a DC source of 6 volts.

(2) Calculate the percentage error that will be encountered if the voltmeter of 1 (a) is used to measure the voltage drop (V_2) across R_2 in the circuit shown in Fig. 9.1 using:

(i) 0-10V range,

(ii) 0-25V range.

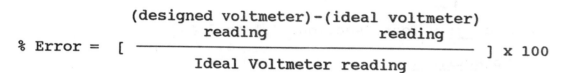

% Error = [(designed voltmeter) - (ideal voltmeter) reading / Ideal Voltmeter reading] x 100

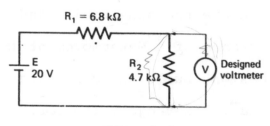

Fig. 9.1

(3) Calculate the percentage error that will be encountered if the milliammeter of 1 (b) is used to measure I_2 in the circuit shown in Fig. 9.2.

202

$R_T = 1500 + \dfrac{30 \times 10}{30 + 10}$

$= 1507.5 \Omega.$

$I = \dfrac{30}{R_T} = 19.99 \text{-}2$

$I_2 = 9.95 \text{mA}$

$Y_1 = \dfrac{9.95 - 9.96}{9.96} = 0.1\%$

$R_T = 1500 + \dfrac{10 \times 10}{10 + 10}$

$= 1505$

$I = \dfrac{30}{1505} = 19.9 \text{mA}. \quad I_2 = \frac{1}{2}I = 9.96 \text{mA}$

Fig. 9.2

(circuit labels: R_s 1.5 kΩ, I_2, I_1, mA Designed ammeter, E 30 V, R_1 10 Ω, R_2 10 Ω)

Prelab Work Space:

a)

$S = 2.5 \text{k}\Omega/\text{volt}$

$R_M = 500 \Omega.$

R_{MULT_1} , R_{MULT_2} , $R_M = 500\Omega.$

$I_M = \dfrac{1}{S}$

$= 2.5^{-1}$

$= 0.4 \text{mA}$

$E = V_{MULT} + V_M$

$E = I_M R_{MULT} + I_M R_M$

$E = I_M (R_{MULT} + R_M)$

when $E = 10V$

$10 = 0.4 \times 10^{-3}(R_{MULT_1} + 500)$

$10 = 0.4 \times 10^{-3} R_{MULT} + 0.2$

$\underline{R_{MULT} = 24.5 \text{k}\Omega}$

when $E = 25V$

$25 = 0.4 \times 10^{-3}(R_{MULT_2} + 500)$

$25 = 0.4 \times 10^{-3} R_{MULT_2} + 0.2$

$R_{MULT_2} = 62 \text{k}\Omega$

(diagram: 24.5kΩ, 62kΩ, R_M)

desgied Vmeter $-0-10V$

(circuit: 6.8k, 20, 4.7k, 24.5k+500)

(circuit: 6.8k, 20V, R_2 3956.222)

$V_2 \left(= \dfrac{20}{6.8 + 3.956k} \right)$ 8956k

$= 7.355V$

$\% \text{Err} = \dfrac{7.355 - 8.1739}{8.1739}$

$= 10\%$

$0 - 25V$

(circuit: 6.8k, 20v, 4.7k, 62k+500)

(circuit: 6.8k, 20v, 4371.279Ω)

$V_2 \left(= \dfrac{20}{6.8 + 4.371k} \right)$ 4.371k

$= 7.82V$

$\% \text{Err} = \dfrac{7.82 - 8.739}{8.751}$

$= 4.32\%$

ACTUAL (ideal) $V \left(= \dfrac{20}{6.8 + 4.7} \right) \cdot 4.7$

$= 8.1739V$

97

b) RANGE 0-10mA

$R_m = 500\Omega$

$I_m > \dfrac{1}{S_M} = \dfrac{1}{2.5k} = 0.4mA$

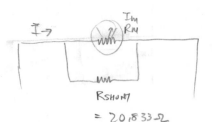

R_{SHUNT}

$= 20.833\Omega$

$R_T = \dfrac{20.833 \times 500}{500 + 20.833}$

$= 20\Omega$

$V_M = I_M R_M$

$= 0.4mA (500)$

$= 0.12V$

$I = I_M + I_{SHUNT}$

$10mA = 40mA + \dfrac{V_M}{R_{SHUNT}}$

$10mA = 0.4mA + \dfrac{0.12}{R_{SHUNT}}$

$R_{SHUNT} = \dfrac{0.12}{9.6 \times 10^{-3}} = 20.833\Omega$

c) $R_{M.S} = 800\Omega$

$E = 6V$

$I_m = \dfrac{1}{S_M} = \dfrac{1}{2.5k} = 0.4mA$

$R_N = 500\Omega$

$V_m = 500(0.4mA)$

$= 0.12V$

$I = \dfrac{E}{R_{IM6}} = \dfrac{6}{800} = 7.5mA$

R_2
773.33Ω

$R_1 \, 28.17\Omega$

R_x

$6V$

$I = I_M + I_1$

$7.5mA = 0.4mA + I_1$

$I_1 = 7.1mA$

$R_1 = \dfrac{V_m}{I_1} = \dfrac{0.12}{7.1mA} = 28.17\Omega$

$R_{IMS} = R_2 + \dfrac{R_M R_1}{R_1 + R_M}$

$800 = R_2 + \dfrac{28.17(500)}{500 + 28.17}$

$R_2 = 800 - 26.66$

$= 773.33\Omega$

9.3 Equipment:

ITEM	MANUFACTURER AND MODEL NO.	LAB. SERIAL NO
DC Power Supply		
VOM meter		
DMM or DC milliammeter		
Metermovement		
Three Decade Resistance Boxes		

Resistors: Two 10 Ω , One 4.7 kΩ and 6.8 kΩ .

9.4 Procedure:

A: Characteristics of Metermovement:

(1) Connect the circuit shown in Fig. 9.3
with resistance R_1 set at its maximum value.

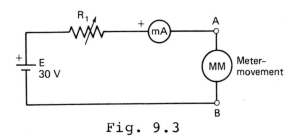

Fig. 9.3

(2) Adjust R_1 until the metermovement (MM)
indicates full-scale deflection (fsd). Measure
and record the current required for full-scale
deflection in Table 9.1.

(3) Connect another decade resistance box (R_2)
across the AB terminals in parallel with the

99

metermovement. Start with $R_2 = 0$ and gradually increase R_2 until the MM indicates half full-scale deflection. [The reading on the milliammeter must be maintained at the same value as in Part 2; R_1 may have to be adjusted.] The value of R_2 is now equal to the internal resistance (R_m) of the metermovement. Record this value in Table 9.1.

Table 9.1

I_{fsd} (mA)	0.4mA
R_m (Ω)	400
Sensitivity of metermovement $$S_m = \frac{1}{I_{fsd}} = k\Omega \ /V$$	SM = 2.5KΩ.

B. Voltmeter design and calibration:

(1) Design a voltmeter with a 0-10V range using the MM of Part A. Check your design calculations with the instructor before proceeding. Show all the calculations and the schematic of the voltmeter circuit. Construct the meter.

$$S = 2.5 k\Omega/V$$

$$I = \frac{1}{S} = 0.4 mA$$

$$E = V_{mult} + V_M$$

$$10 = I_m R_{mult} + I_M R_M$$

$$10 = 0.4 mA\, R_{mult} + 0.4 mA\,(400)$$

$$R_{mult} = 24.6 K\Omega.$$

(2) To calibrate the 'designed voltmeter', use the VOM or DMM as a standard voltmeter. Set up the circuit as shown in Fig. 9.4 and for various values of E, read and record the values of the readings of both meters in Table 9.2.

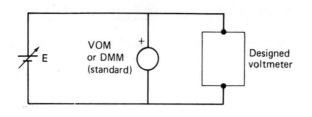

Fig. 9.4

Table 9.2

$V_{Standard}$ (Volts)	$V_{designed}$ (Volts)	% Error
0	0	0
1	1	0
2	2	0
3	3	0
4	4	0
5	5	0
6	5.9	1.67
7	6.9	1.42
8	7.89	1.37
9	8.89	1.22
10	9.99	0.1%

(3) Plot the "calibration chart" (designed-voltmeter reading versus standard-meter reading) on Graph 9.1.

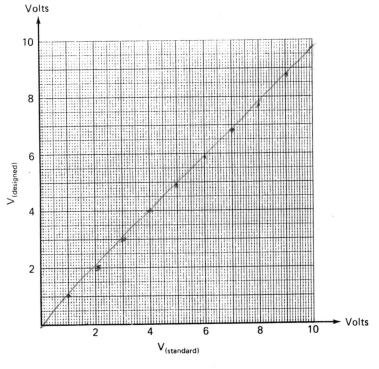

Graph 9.1

(4) Set up the circuit as in Fig. 9.1. Measure the voltage across R_2 using the "designed-voltmeter". Calculate the percentage error of the meter assuming the theoretical value of V_2 as being the standard value.

% Error =

$V = 7.37v.$

$$V_1 = \frac{7.37 - 7.355}{7.355} \times 100$$

$$= 0.2\%$$

(5) Design and construct a voltmeter with 0-25V range using MM of Part A. Show the schematic of the meter circuit.

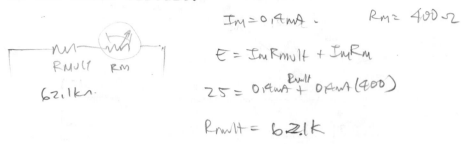

RMULT   RM

62.1kₙ.

$I_M = 0.4mA$. $R_M = 400\Omega$

$E = I_M R_{mult} + I_M R_M$

$25 = 0.4mA \overset{R_{mult}}{+} 0.4mA (400)$

$R_{mult} = 62.1k$

(6) Set up the circuit as in Fig. 9.1 and measure the voltage across R_2 using the above "designed-voltmeter". Calculate the percentage error of this meter.

% Error =

$V_{metr} = 8v$

$\% \quad \dfrac{8 - 7.355}{7.355} \times 100$

$= 8.76.$

104

C.   Ammeter design and calibration:

(1)   Design a milliammeter with a 0-10 mA
range using the MM of Part A. Check your
design with the instructor before proceeding.
Draw the schematic of the ammeter circuit.
Construct the meter.

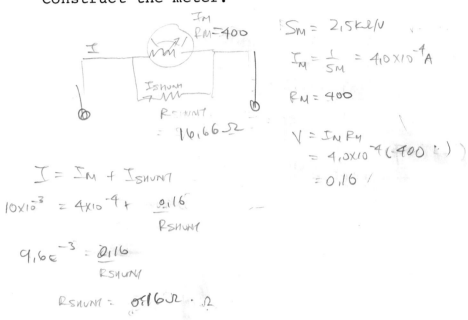

$S_M = 2.5 k\Omega/V$

$I_M = \frac{1}{S_M} = 4.0 \times 10^{-4} A$

$R_M = 400$

$V = I_N R_M$
$= 4.0 \times 10^{-4} (400 \ ))$
$= 0.16$

$I = I_M + I_{SHUNT}$

$10 \times 10^{-3} = 4 \times 10^{-4} + \frac{0.16}{R_{SHUNT}}$

$9.6e^{-3} = \frac{0.16}{R_{SHUNT}}$

$R_{SHUNT} = 0.16\Omega \cdot \Omega$

(2)   To calibrate the 'designed milliammeter', use
the DMM or milliammeter as the 'standard
meter'. Set up the circuit as shown in
Fig. 9.5. Vary the current supplied from
the source (by varying R) in steps of 1 mA.
Record the 'standard milliammeter' and
'designed-milliammeter' readings in
Table 9.4.

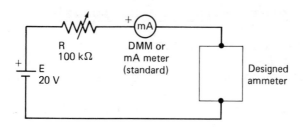

Fig. 9.5

Table 9.4

$I_{Standard}$ (mA)	$I_{designed}$ (mA)	% Accuracy
0	0	0
1	1	0
2	2	0
3	2.9	3.33
4	3.7	2.5
5	4.8	4%
6	5.8	3.3
7	6.4	8.6
8	7.3	8.7
9	8.2	8.9
10	9.1	9

(3) Plot the "calibration chart" of the designed
    meter on Graph 9.2.

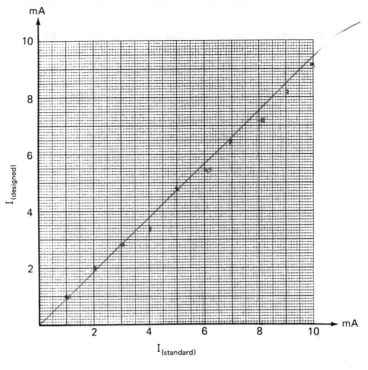

Graph 9.2

(4) Set up the circuit as in Fig. 9.2. Use the
    "designed-milliammeter" to measure the current
    through R_2. Assuming the theoretical value of I_2 as
    being the standard value, calculate the percentage
    error of the meter.

     % Error =

D. **Design and calibration of an Ohmmeter:**

(1) Note the mid-scale ohmic value of your MM; design an ohmmeter with this midscale ohmic value using a DC source of 6V. Show all the calculations and schematic of the ohmmeter circuit. Check your design with the instructor before proceeding.

$$I_{f,s} = \frac{1}{s} = \frac{1}{2.5k} = 40mA$$

$$R_M = 500\Omega$$

$$E = 10V$$

$$R.M.S = ?$$

$$R_{N.S} = 800\Omega$$

$$I_M = 0.4mA$$

$$V_M = 500(0.4mA)$$
$$= 0.2V$$

$$I = \frac{E}{R_{1M}} = \frac{6}{800} = 7.5mA$$

$$I = I_m + I_1$$
$$7.5mA = 0.4mA + I_1$$
$$I_1 = 7.1(mA)$$
$$R_1 = \frac{V_M}{I_1} = \frac{0.2}{7.1mA} = 28.17\Omega$$

$$R_{MS} = R_2 + \frac{R_M R_1}{R_1 + R_M}$$

$$800 = R_2 + \frac{500(28.17)}{500 + 28.17}$$

$$R_2 = 773.33\Omega$$

108

(2) To calibrate the 'designed-ohmmeter', use a
     decade resistance box as a <u>standard resistor</u>
     and set up the circuit as shown in Fig. 9.6.

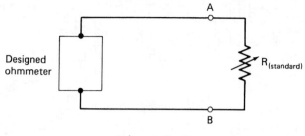

Fig. 9.6

(3) Short-circuit the A-B terminals (R = 0) and
     note the deflection on the 'designed-ohmmeter'
     (do not adjust any resistances). Remove the
     short-circuit and vary the values of R as
     shown in Table 9.5; measure the corresponding
     values of R using the 'designed- ohmmeter'.

Table 9.5

R$_{standard}$ (Ω)	R (Ω) (designed meter)
O	O
50	40
200	180
500	475
800	750
1000	900
2000	1800
3000	2860
5000	4500
8000	7000
10000	5000

(4) Plot the 'calibration chart' of the designed

ohmmeter on Graph 9.3.

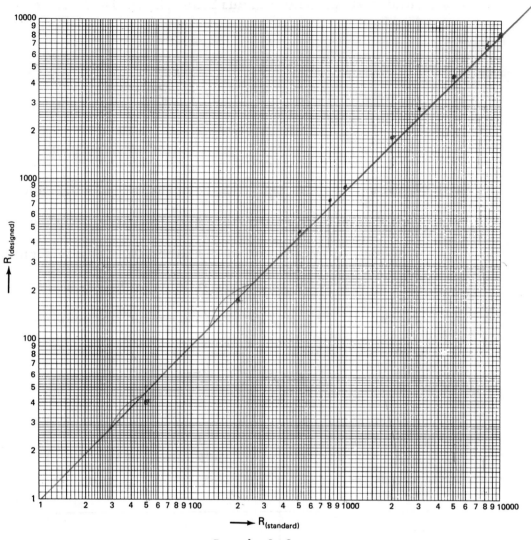

Graph 9.3

9.5   Comments and Conclusions:

1. What is the voltage drop across the MM at the

full-scale deflection?

The voltage drop a $I_{f.s}$

Was $U = I_{f_s} \cdot R_M$

$= 0.4 mA \; (400 \, \Omega)$

$= 0.16 V$

2. Is there a relationship between the
    sensitivity (S_m) and the internal resistance
    (R_m) of the metermovement? Explain.

$$S_m = \frac{1}{I_{fs}}$$

S_m is the inverse of the Internal resistance of the meter movement, at full scale current.

3. What is the sensitivity of the 'designed-
    voltmeter' as compared to that of the
    metermovement. The sensitivity of the metermovement is $2.5 k\Omega/V$ where as the which is the same as the designed voltmeter.

4. What is the sensitivity of the VOM that you
    used as a standard meter?

    $2.5 k\Omega/V$

5. If, in the circuit of Fig. 9.1, R_1 and R_2 are respectively 68 Ω and 47 Ω , instead of 6.8 kΩ and 4.7 kΩ , what is the loading effect of the 'designed-voltmeter' on 10V range?

(Calculate the % accuracy of the meter reading.)

The loading effect with a series resistor will cause the designed Voltmeter to have a better accuracy.

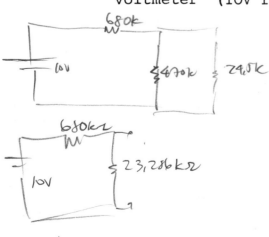

$I_{ideal} = 86.95 mA$

$V = 4.08665 V$

$I_{design} = 87.02 mA$

$V = 4.08 V$

% error low

6. If, in the circuit of Fig. 9.1, $R_1 = 680$ kΩ and $R_2 = 470$ kΩ instead of 6.8 kΩ and 4.7 kΩ , calculate the loading effect of the 'designed-voltmeter' (10V range).

680k

470k   24.5k

10V

680kΩ

23.286kΩ

10V

$V_{AB} = \dfrac{10}{680 + 23.2866k} \times 23.286k$

$= 6.33 V$

% error $\dfrac{0.33 - 4.08}{4.08} = 789\%$

7. What is the sensitivity of the lab-constructed
    milliammeter as compared with that of the
    metermovement?

    *The sensitivity of the lab constructed
    milliammeter is the same of that
    of the metermovement.*

8. A milliammeter with an accuracy of ± 2% reads
    3.5 mA when set on the 10 mA range. Within
    what range of values (about 3.5 mA) is this
    meter accurate?

    *The milliammeter is good within
    the ranges of 3,57mA and 3,93mA*

9. The accuracy of any milliammeter is related to
    the correct value of the shunt resistance
    (R_{sh}). Consider a nominal 10 mA range
    milliammeter which consists of a metermovement
    with the following parameters:

    $$S_m = 2.5 \text{ k}\Omega \text{ /V; } R_m = 500 \text{ }\Omega$$

Assume that the value of R_{sh} used, turns out to be 20 Ω (incorrect value). Calculate the percentage error of this milliammeter. Does this milliammeter read too high or too low?

$I = I_m + I_s$.

$10mA = 0.4mA + \dfrac{0.2}{20}$

$10mA \leq 10.4mA$

$I_m = \dfrac{1}{S_m} = 0.4mA$

$V = I_m R_m$

$= 0.4mA \times 500$

$= 0.2V$

Ideal $= 10mA$

design $= 10.4mA$

$\% = \dfrac{10.4 - 10}{10} \times 100$

$= 4\%$.

∴ It reads too high.

10. Summarize the advantages and disadvantages
of measuring an unknown resistance by the
three different methods you have used in the
lab. (Volt-amp method, Wheatstone bridge and
Ohmmeter.)

— using volt-amp method, errors come into play
because of meter loads. It is easier than others
— Ohmeter are easy to use, but the accuracy
is not always perfect
— a wheatstone bridge is probably the most
accurate, but difficult to construct.

11. The Ohmmeter readings are more accurate around
the mid-scale range and less accurate at the
extreme ends of the scale. Explain why.

The scales for an ohmmeter are logarithmic
scales. It is very difficult to read
the scale when it is above or below
the midscale region.

115

12. What is the purpose of the 'zero-adjust' potentiometer on the VOM (as an ohmmeter)?

As the source of the ohmmeter dies, the ohmmeter becomes less accurate. The potentiometer is to calibrate it back to the original accuracy.

13. Why is the 'ohm' scale non-linear and counter-clockwise?

When there is no resistance in a circuit, the full scale current travels through the meter so that the source & vice-versa. The meter is also most sensitive around the centre when resistance becomes very high the current is very small, so the scale must be exponential.

No resistance scale reads full scale. as we add more resistance the current drops and therefore the scale drop causing an reading of counter clockwise

10 | THE OSCILLOSCOPE AS A CURRENT AND VOLTAGE MEASURING INSTRUMENT

Required Reading: Text, section 7.5

10.1   **Objective:**

- To gain familiarity with the basic operating

  controls of a dual-beam oscilloscope.

- To use the oscilloscope for measuring voltages
  and currents.

10.2   **Prelab Assignment:**

Read the operating instructions for the

dual-beam oscilloscope available at your

laboratory. Appendix 10.1 shows, as an example,

the operating instructions for the Philips PM-3233

oscilloscope.

10.3   Equipment:

ITEM	MANUFACTURER AND MODEL NO.	LAB. SERIAL NO
Dual-Beam Oscilloscope		
Signal Generator		
DC Power Supply		
DMM or VOM		
Decade Resistance Box		

Resistors: One 10 Ω

10.4   Procedure:

A.   <u>Calibration of the Oscilloscope:</u>

(1)   Turn on the oscilloscope after you have become familiar with the locations and functions of its controls.

(2)   Set (Time/div) to 0.1 m sec/div and (trigger mode) to (Auto). Adjust the focus and intensity controls to achieve well-defined time-base line displays (one for each beam).

(3)   Adjust the vertical-position control to center each beam on the screen; set the (AC - 0 - DC) controls to (AC).

(4) Connect the Cal-terminal of the
oscilloscope to the input of channel Y_A.
[The Cal-terminal output provides a
square waveform with a well-defined
(peak-to-peak) voltage.] Adjust the
vertical sensitivity of Y_A (V/div) to
achieve maximum vertical deflection of
the display. Measure the (peak-to-peak)
deflection and determine V (p-p).

(5) Repeat Step # 4 for channel Y_B and
record your results in Table 10.1.

Table 10.1

Channel #	(p-p) deflection (div)	Sensitivity (V/div)	V (p-p) (V)
Y_A	6	6,1	0,6V
Y_B	6	0,1	0,6V

How do the V (p-p) values compare with
V (p-p) of the (Cal) output?

B. Voltage Measurement:

(1) Use the VOM (or DMM) to adjust the
terminal voltage (V_T) of the DC power
supply to 1V.

119

(2) Set the (AC - 0 - DC) control of Y_A to (DC). Connect Y_A to display the terminal voltage of the DC power supply [adjust (V/div) to achieve the maximum vertical deflection]; determine the DC-voltage and record in Table 10.2.

(3) Repeat the above steps for each value of V_T in Table 10.2.

Table 10.2

V_T (V)	1	2	5	10
Vertical Deflection (div)	1	2	2.5	2
Vertical Sensitivity (V/div)	1	1	2	5
Measured Voltage by the oscilloscope V_{osc} (V)	1	2	5	10V

(4) Plot the measured voltage by the oscilloscope V_{osc} versus V_T on Graph 10.1.

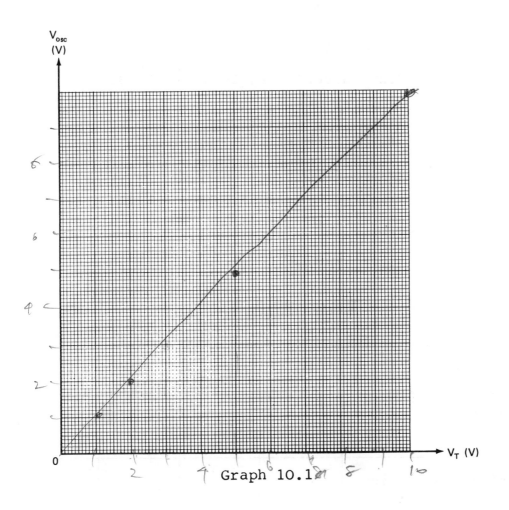

Graph 10.1

C. Current Measurement:

   (1) Connect the circuit shown in Fig. 10.1.
        Set V_T to 10V and adjust the decade
        resistance box (R_X) to 10 kΩ . Connect
        Y_A to display the voltage across the
        10 Ω -current-sampling resistance
        [Y_A now displays 10 X I]. Adjust the
        vertical sensitivity of Y_A to achieve
        the maximum vertical deflection;
        determine the DC-current and record your
        results in Table 10.3.

121

(2)   Repeat the above measurement for each of

the values of R_X in Table 10.3.

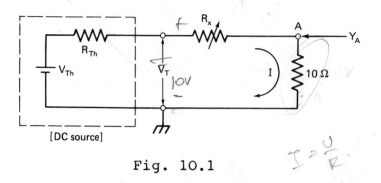

Fig. 10.1

$$I = \frac{v}{R}$$

Table 10.3

R_X (k Ω)	10	5	2	1
I (mA)	1 mA	2 mA	5 mA	10 mA
Vertical Deflection (div)	5	4	2.5	2
Vertical Sensitivity (V/div)	2 mV	5 mV	20 mV	50 mV
Measured Current by the oscilloscope I_{osc} (mA)	10 mV	20 mV	50 mV	100 mV

(3)   Plot the measured current by the

oscilloscope I_{osc} versus I on Graph

10.2.

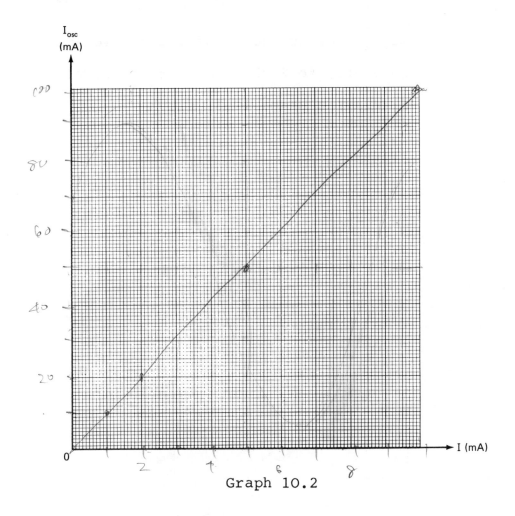

Graph 10.2

D. <u>Signal Display:</u>

(1) Adjust the frequency of the (sinusoidal) signal generator to 1 kHz. Set the vertical sensitivity of Y_A to 1V/div and the (Time/div) control to 0.1 msec/div. Connect Y_A to display the terminal voltage V_T of the sinusoidal generator; adjust V_T to achieve a (peak-to-peak) display of 8V.

(2) Plot V_T versus time on Graph 10.3.

123

(3) Adjust the frequency of the sinusoidal generator to 2 kHz and plot the resulting display on Graph 10.3.

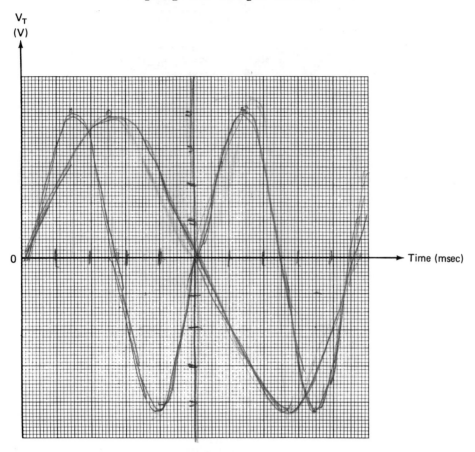

Graph 10.3

10.5 Comments and Conclusions:

1. What is the maximum possible voltage that can be measured with your oscilloscope?

   The maximum voltage measured is for peak-peak

2. Assume that a minimum deflection of 0.1 of a division can be estimated accurately. What is the minimum voltage that can be accurately measured by your oscilloscope?

   The minimum voltage would be 0.02 volts.

124

3. Consider the circuit shown in Fig. 10.2. Assume that the input resistance of Y_A is 1 MΩ and the vertical sensitivity is set at 0.2V/div. Determine:

a. the number of vertical-divisions of the corresponding beam deflection.

b. the voltage measured by the oscilloscope.

c. the voltage measured by the oscilloscope, assuming that the input resistance of Y_A is increased to 10 MΩ .

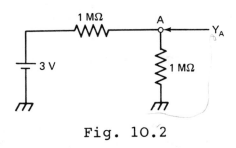

Fig. 10.2

a) 5 divisions in the scope

b) the voltage is 1 volt

c) The new voltage would be 1-49 volts

Philips (PM-3233) Oscilloscope   *Courtesy, Philips Electronics Ltd.*

CONTROLS AND SOCKETS

X POSITION (R1)   Continuously variable control giving
                       horizontal positioning of the display.

MAGN' (SK1)   Incorporates a switch for calibrated 5x
                       magnification of the time base.

TIME/cm (SK2)   Time-coefficient control of the
                       time-base; 21 way switch with a position
                       for external X deflection (X via Y_A).

CAL.-TIME/cm (R2/SK3)
                       Continuously variable control of the time
                       coefficients.
                       In the CAL. position the time-coefficient
                       is calibrated.

LEVEL (R3)   Continuously variable control to select
                       the level at which the time-base
                       generator starts.

CAL. (BU1)	Outlet for square-wave voltage of 600 mV p-p for calibration purposes.

TRIGGERING (SK4..13)

Controls for trigger source, slope and mode; 10-way push-button switch.

Y_A (SK4)	Internal triggering signal derived from channel Y_A.
Y_B (SK5)	Internal triggering signal derived from channel Y_B.
EXT. (SK6)	Triggering signal derived from a voltage applied to the TRIGG. input socket.
MAINS (SK7)	Triggering signal derived from an internal voltage with mains frequency. This trigger source is inoperative when the instrument is supplied with an external DC voltage.
+ (SK8)	Provides for triggering on the positive slope of the signal.
- (SK9)	Provides for triggering on the negative slope of the signal.
AUTO (SK10)	Provides for a free-running time-base in the absence of triggering signals and automatic signal-derived limitation on the LEVEL control range.
AC (SK11)	Triggering with coupling capacitor in triggering-signal path.
DC (SK12)	Direct coupling for triggering on a slowly varying voltage or for full-bandwidth working.
TV (SK13)	Enables triggering on either line or frame pulses of TV signals, as dictated by the position of TIME/cm switch SK2. Triggering on frame pulses in positions 50 μs/cm to 0.5 s/cm and on line pulses in position 0.2 μs/cm to 20 μs/cm.
TRIGG. (BU2)	Input BNC socket for external triggering signals.

BEAM SELECTOR A (SK 14)

If this push-button is depressed, vertical deflection is achieved by the signal connected to the channel Y_A input.

BEAM SELECTOR A (SK 15)

If this push-button is depressed, vertical deflection is achieved by the signal connected to the channel Y_B input.

If both switch A (SK 14) and switch B (SK 15) are depressed, vertical deflection is achieved by both the signal connected to the channel Y_A input and the signal connected to the channel Y_B input.

AC-O-DC (SK 16 & 19)

Signal coupling, three position switch.
AC : via coupling capacitor
O   : interruption of connection between input socket and input circuit, the latter being earthed.
DC : Direct coupling

AMPL. (SK 17 & 18)   Control of the vertical deflection coefficients, 12-way switch.

CAL.-AMPL. (R4 & 5)   Continuously variable control of the vertical deflection coefficients. In the CAL. position, the deflection coefficient is calibrated.

DC BAL. (R6 & 7)   Continuously variable control of the direct-voltage balance of the vertical amplifier.

ILLUM. (SK 20 & R8)   Continuously variable control of the graticule illumination. Incorporates mains switch.

FOCUS (R9)   Continuously variable control of the electron-beam focusing.

INTENS (R10)   Continuously variable control of the trace brilliance.

1 MOhm-20 pF (BU3 & 5)

Input BNC socket for the vertical deflection signals.

POSITION (R11 & 12)

Continuously variable control giving vertical positioning of the display.

(BU4)   Earth socket.

TRIGGERING

General

In order to obtain a stationary trace, the horizontal deflection must always be started at a fixed point of the signal. The time-base generator is, therefore started by narrow trigger pulses formed in the trigger pulse shaper (Schmitt trigger), controlled by a signal originating from the vertical input signal or an external source.

Trigger coupling

AC   If the signal voltage contains a DC component triggering can cease when the level potentiometer cannot supply the correct DC level for the Schmitt trigger. In this case it is useful to apply AC coupling. AC coupling is obtained by inserting a capacitor in the trigger path. This means that the signal can still be DC coupled to the Y channels.

DC   DC Coupling is useful when the mean value of this signal varies. This sort of signal often occurs in digital systems. With AC coupling the trigger point would not be fixed which would give rise to jitter or even loss of triggering.

Trigger level

In case of a complicated signal in which a number of non-identical voltage shapes occur periodically, the time axis should always be started with the same voltage shape so as to obtain a stationary trace. This is possible when one of the details has a deviating amplitude. By means of the LEVEL knob, the trigger level can be set in such a way that only this larger voltage variation passes this level. The LEVEL control is also very useful when two signals must be compared accurately e.g. in phase measurements. By means of the LEVEL control the starting point of the traces can then be shifted exactly on to the central graticule line.

Automatic triggering

Automatic triggering (when the AUTO switch is depressed) is most often used on account of its simple operation.
In this mode it is possible to display a large variety of waveforms having different amplitude and shape, without it being necessary to operate any of the trigger controls.
If no triggering signal is present, a time-base line remains visible on the screen. This is useful for zero reference purposes. In this trigger mode the level can be adjusted over the peak-to-peak value of the AC component of the

signal. If none of the switches AUTO, AC, DC or TV is
depressed, the oscilloscope works in the automatic mode, but
with the entire level range available. This has the
advantage that there is always a trace visible, even when no
TRIGG. push-buttons are depressed.

External triggering

External triggering is applied for signals having a strongly
varying amplitude, if a signal having a fixed amplitude and
equal frequency is available. Even more important is
external triggering in case of complex signals and pulse
patterns. Then external triggering can be used to avoid
double traces.
This obviates the necessity of readjusting the level setting
at every variation of the input signal.

Triggering with the mains frequency

In this case the triggering signal is a sine-wave with the
mains frequency. This trigger source is useful if the
frequency of the signal under observation is coupled with the
mains frequency.
It is, e.g., possible to recognize the hum component of a
signal by triggering on that component.

Triggering with television signals

It is possible to trigger on the line or frame sync pulses of
television signals. In positions .5 s to 50 μs of the
TIME/cm switch triggering takes place on the frame sync
pulses and in positions 20 μs to .2 μs on the line sync
pulses of the signal.
The position of the trigger slope switches must correspond to
the polarity of the video information of the signal.

TIME-BASE MAGNIFIER

The magnifier is operated with a push-pull switch.
When this switch is in the x5 position, the time-base sweep
speed is increased 5 times. In this position the sweep time
is determined by dividing the indicated TIME/cm value by 5.

Z MODULATION

In order to bring extra information in the C.R.T. display
without changing the form of the display, the brightness of
the trace can be lowered by an externally applied voltage.
The external signal must, therefore, be fed to the Z MOD
socket at the rear of the oscilloscope.
The voltage required for visible brightness modulation
depends on the position of the INTENS control.
With an average brightness of the trace, a 20 V_{p-p} voltage
is amply sufficient for obtaining a good visible "Z-modulation".

THE DUAL-BEAM TUBE

The cathode-ray tube used in PM 3233 oscilloscope is a
dual-beam tube in which two beams are generated in one gun
and can be deflected independently.
This arrangement is also known as split-beam tube.

In this tube, both time-base lines are exactly in parallel as
they originate from one point and are under the influence of
one common horizontal amplifier. Because the two traces
originate from one gun, they show little distortion in
relation to one another.

The split-beam tube is very suitable for displaying signals
with a low repetition rate at relatively fast sweep speeds,
since it may be regarded as a tube with a chopper and an
infinitely high chopper frequency.

For equalizing and adjusting the brightness of both beams,
two magnets are mounted symmetrically on the C.R.T. One of
these magnets can be readjusted by means of a screwdriver
through an opening in the bottom-plate of the oscilloscope.

. BRIEF CHECKING PROCEDURE

STARTING POSITIONS OF THE CONTROLS

- Push-buttons Y_A SK4, + SK8 and BEAM SELECTOR A SK14 & B
  SK 15 depressed.
- TIME/cm switch SK2 to .1 ms
- AMPL switches SK 17 & SK 18 to .1 V/cm
- MAGN switch SK 1 to x1
- POSITION potentiometers R1, R11 and R12 to their
  mid-positions
- INTENS potentiometer R10 fully clockwise
- TIME/cm and AMPL potentiometers R2, R4 and R5 to CAL

Unless otherwise stated, the controls always occupy the same
position as in the previous check.

11 THE OSCILLOSCOPE FOR SIGNALS DISPLAY

Required Reading: Text, section 7.5

11.1 Objective:

- To gain familiarity with the triggering and synchronization controls of the oscilloscope.

- To examine the effects of circuit ground on signals display.

11.2 Prelab Assignment:

(1) A sinusoidal signal of 400 Hz is to be displayed on the oscilloscope, using channel Y_A, such that:

- two complete cycles of the signal are to appear on the screen

- the starting-point of the display is a positive-slope zero-crossing point

133

What are the proper settings for:

- the (trigger-source) control, *YA*
- the (Time/div) control, and *0,5/cm*
- the (level) control? *adjust zero cross.*

(2)   Consider the circuit shown in Fig. 11.1. A dual-beam oscilloscope is used to display the voltage differences between the various nodes of the circuit. Initially the time-base lines for both beams are set at the center of the screen; the vertical sensitivities for Y_A and Y_B are set at 1V/div. The (Time/div) control is set at 1 msec./div.

Plot the resulting displays of both beams, for each of the following conditions.

Condition #	Y_A at node #	Y_B at node #	Ground at node #
1	x	y	z
2	x	z	y
3	z	y	x

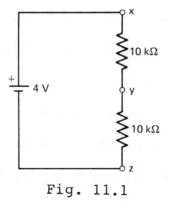

Fig. 11.1

Prelab Work Space:

Prelab Work Space:

11.3   Equipment:

ITEM	MANUFACTURER AND MODEL NO.	LAB. SERIAL NO
Dual-Beam Oscilloscope		
Signal Generator		
DC Power Supply		
DMM or VOM		
Decade Resistance Box		

Resistors: Two 10 k Ω

136

11.4 Procedure:

A.   Signal Display and Synchronization:

(1)   Set the controls of the oscilloscope to the following positions:

Triggering-source.........Y_B

   -mode   ....Auto

   -slope ....(+)

Time/div ....0.5 msec/div (calib.)

For both beams:

vertical sensitivity ...   1V/div (calib.)

(AC-O-DC) control ......   (0)

Y-position ....   center of screen

(2)   Connect the <u>time-base</u> output terminal (usually located at the back panel of the oscilloscope) to Y_A.   Set the (AC-O-DC) control of Y_A to (DC).   The A-beam now displays <u>one cycle</u> of the sawtooth waveform from the internal sweep generator.

(3)   Adjust the (X-position) control to move the starting point of the display to the extreme left-hand vertical graticule line. Plot the display on Graph 11.1.

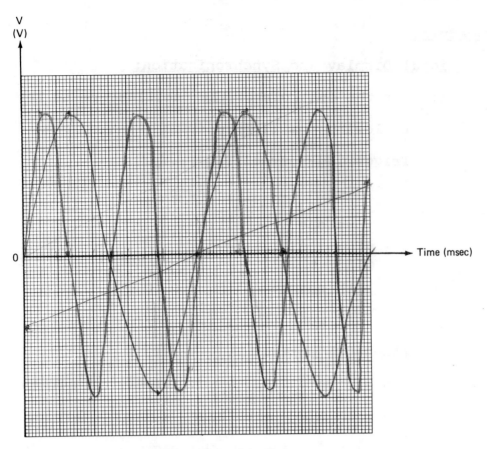

Graph 11.1

(4) Adjust the frequency of the sinusoidal-
signal generator to 400 Hz; connect Y_B to
display the terminal voltage V_T of the
generator. Set the (AC-O-DC) control of
Y_B to (AC) and adjust V_T to achieve a
peak-to-peak display of 6V.

(5) Vary the position of the (level) control
and observe its effect on the displays of
both beams. Comment on your results.

Level control moves the
frequency curve left and
right to help align the waves.

138

(6)   Adjust the (level) control until the
       starting (extreme left-hand) point of the
       Y_B display is a positive-slope
       zero-crossing point. Plot the display of
       Y_B on Graph 11.1.

(7)   Set the triggering slope to (-); how
       does this change affect the displays?

       the (−) trigger inverts the
       display giving a −ve slope

(8)   Set the triggering mode to free running
       and vary the (level) control. How does
       this change affect the displays?

       positive slope at the origin
       level control is a manual control
       of the triggers

(9)   Set the triggering mode and slope back
       to (Auto) and (+), respectively. Adjust
       the (Time/div) control to 1 msec/div.
       How does this change affect the displays
       and how many trigger pulses does the
       sweep generator ignore during each sweep
       cycle?

       increases the number of cycles.
       in the display.

B.   **Effects of Circuit Ground:**

(1)   Connect the circuit shown in Fig.

11.2. Use the VOM (or DMM) to adjust

V_T to 4V.

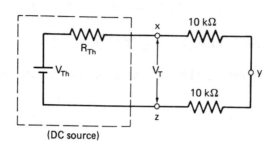

Fig. 11.2

(2)   Set both (AC-0-DC) controls to (DC).

Connect Y_A to node x, Y_B to node y and

the oscilloscope ground terminal to

node z. Measure V_x and V_y w.r.t. node z

and record your results in Table 11.1.

(3)   Repeat Step # 2 for each of the

conditions indicated in Table 11.1.

Table 11.1

Y_A @ node #	Y_B @ node #	ground @ node #	V_x (V)	V_y (V)	V_z (V)	w.r.t. node #
x	y	z	4v	2.25	0	z
x	z	y	2v	0	−2√	y
z	y	x	0	−4	−2√	x

(4) Connect the circuit shown in Fig.
11.3; set V_T to 25 V. The circuit has a
fixed ground connection that is common
with the oscilloscope ground. Use your
oscilloscope [WITH THE GROUND-TERMINAL OF
THE OSCILLOSCOPE PERMANENTLY CONNECTED TO
THE CIRCUIT GROUND] to determine the
voltages across the source terminals
V_T, R_1, R_2 and R_3. Record your results
in Table 11.2.

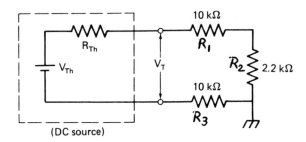

Fig. 11.3

Table 11.2

v_T (V)	v_{R_1} (V)	v_{R_2} (V)	v_{R_3} (V)
25 v	11.25	2.5	11.25

12 | THE OSCILLOSCOPE AS A CURVE TRACER

12.1   Objective:

.   To examine the XY-mode operation of the
         oscilloscope.

.   To display the I-V characteristics of
         two-terminal devices.

12.2 (a)   Introduction:

         Experiment #1 dealt with the I-V
characteristics of a resistor. The characteristics
were obtained by taking a number of measurements of
the voltage across and the current through the
resistor, at different settings of the source
voltage. This procedure is rather tedious and time
consuming.

         A quick and a more accurate method of
obtaining the I-V characteristics involves the use
of an oscilloscope together with a sweep voltage
source as shown in Fig. 12.1.

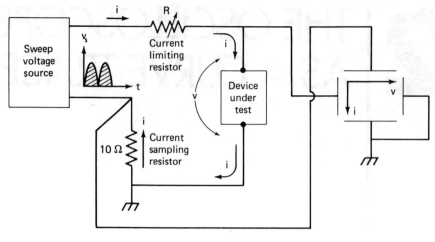

Fig. 12.1

The voltage across the current-sampling resistor is applied to the vertical-deflecting plates of the scope; hence, the vertical position of the electron beam is directly proportional to "i." Similarly, the voltage across the device is applied to the horizontal-deflecting plates; therefore, the horizontal position of the beam is directly proportional to "v." Thus, v & i control the x and y coordinates of the electron beam. A change in the value of the sweep voltage, v_s, will lead to a new set of coordinates for the I-V characteristics, displayed on the screen of the oscilloscope.

The sweep voltage must satisfy three basic requirements here:

(a)   it must be repetitive to ensure retracing of the I-V graph.

(b)   its repetition rate must be sufficiently fast to avoid any flickering effect.

(c)   it must have a continuous amplitude range

(square wave is no good).

The current-limiting resistor, R, is there to

ensure the safety of the device under test.

12.2 (b)   <u>Prelab Assignment</u>:

Given the I-V characteristics of a two-

terminal device as shown in Fig. 12.2:

(1)   determine graphically (using the load-line

approach) the coordinates (V & I) of the

operating point for the following settings of

the source voltage:

0, ± 1, ± 2V.

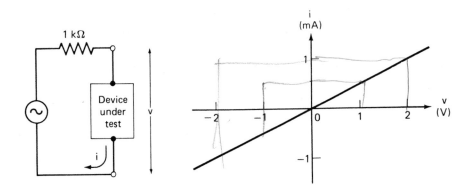

Fig. 12.2

$(0v, 0mA)$ $(1v, \frac{1}{2}mA)$ $(2v, 1mA$

$(-1v, -\frac{1}{2}mA))$ $(-2v, -1mA)$

Prelab Work Space:

12.3   **Equipment:**

ITEM	MANUFACTURER AND MODEL NO.	LAB. SERIAL NO
Dual-Beam Oscilloscope		
Signal Generator		

Resistors: One 1 kΩ & 10 kΩ

Diodes: IN4001 (or equivalent)

12.4   **Procedure:**

A.   **Setting the Oscilloscope in the XY-Mode:**

(1)   Set the appropriate control of your oscilloscope to allow access to the input terminals of the X-amplifier. For example, setting the (Time/div) control of the Philips PM3233 Oscilloscope at "X via Y_A" converts Y_A to be the input terminals of the X-amplifier (X-input), i.e., any signal applied now to Y_A will control the X-position of beam B [beam A does not exist in the XY-mode].

(2)   Set the controls for Y_B as follows:

. vertical sensitivity .... 2 mV/div

. (AC-O-DC) .... (O)

(YA) Set the controls for X-input at:

. sensitivity.................. 0.5V/div

. (AC-O-DC).................... (O)

(3) Adjust the (Y_B-position) and the
(X-position) controls to place the beam
at the center of the screen; the beam YX-
coordinates are now considered as (0, 0).

B. Obtaining the I-V Characteristics for

Two-Terminal Devices:

(1) Adjust the frequency of the sinusoidal
generator to about 200 Hz. Use the
oscilloscope to adjust the terminal
voltage of the generator (V_T) to 4V
(peak-to-peak).

(2) Connect the circuit shown in Fig. 12.3;
the two-terminal device under test is a
1 kΩ resistor.

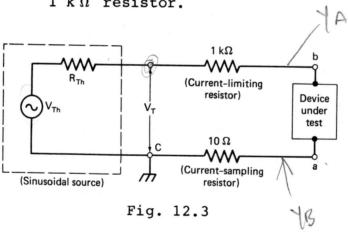

Fig. 12.3

(3) Connect node (a) to the Y_B-input,
node (b) to the X-input and node (c) to
the oscilloscope ground terminal. Set
both (AC-O-DC) controls to (DC). The X
and Y deflections of the beam (w.r.t. the
center of the screen) represent the
voltage across and 10X the current

148

through the device, respectively.

(4) Plot the I-V characteristics of the device under test on Graph 12.1.

(5) Repeat the above steps for each of the following devices:

. a 10 k Ω resistor

. a semiconductor diode (IN4001 or equivalent).

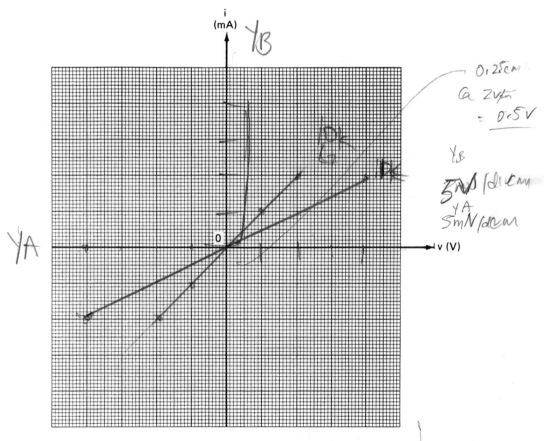

Graph 12.1

$R = \dfrac{V}{I} = \dfrac{5 V/cm}{5 \times 10^{-7}/cm} = 10 k \Omega$

$I = 5mV/dw \div 10$

$= 5 \times 10^{-7} v/cm$

0.25cm
@ 2v/t
= 0.5V

Y.B
5mV/d1cm
YA
5mV/dcm

$R = \dfrac{U}{I} = \dfrac{1U}{10mV/_{/6}} = 1000k$

12.5   <u>Comments and Conclusions:</u>

1.   What is the "inherent" error in the procedure
      for displaying the I-V characteristics?

   The largest source of error
   is reading the small division
   on the oscilloscope. Parallax
   errors plays a large role
   in these errors.

2.   Suppose that the source in Fig. 12.3 is a
      floating source, where would you connect the
      oscilloscope-ground terminal in order to
      display more accurately the I-V
      characteristics of any two-terminal device?
      Sketch the resulting display for a 1 kΩ
      resistor?

   You would connect the ground
   potential at a common point
   in the origin (to all amplifiers)

3. How is the I-V display of the semiconductor
    diode, Graph 12.1, affected by doubling the
    value of the current-limited resistance?
    Sketch the resulting display.

4. How is the I-V display of the 1 k Ω resistor,
    Graph 12.1, affected by doubling the (peak-
    to-peak) value of V_T? Sketch the resulting
    display.

13 | TRANSIENTS IN RC-CIRCUITS

Required Reading: Text, section 8.5

13.1   Objective:

To investigate the transient behaviour of simple RC-circuits.

13.2   Prelab Assignment:

Consider the circuit shown in Fig. 13.1. The switch S was in position (a) for a long time and then moved to position (b) at t = o. For each of the combinations of R & C shown in Table 13.1, determine:

(1)   the circuit's time constant, τ ,

(2)   the initial charging current, $i_C(o^+)$.

Table 13.1

Combination #	R [kΩ]	C [μF]
1	1	0.01
2	1	0.02
3	2	0.01

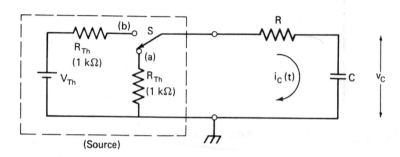

Fig. 13.1

Prelab Work Space:

1) time constant
= total series resistance × capacitance value

1. $T_c = 1000 \times (1 \times 10^{-8})$
$= 1 \times 10^{-5}$ s

2. $T_c = 1000 \times (2 \times 10^{-8})$
$= 2 \times 10^{-5}$ s

3. $T_c = 2000 \times (1 \times 10^{-8})$
$= 2 \times 10^{-5}$ s

154

Prelab Work Space:

$$\dot{c}(o^t) = \frac{E}{R_1}$$ $$① = \frac{V_t}{R_{th} + R_1}$$ $$② \;\frac{V_{ar}}{R_{th} + R_1}$$ $$③ \;\frac{V_{ar}}{R_{var} + R_1}$$

13.3   Equipment:

ITEM	MANUFACTURER AND MODEL NO.	LAB. SERIAL NO
Dual-Beam Oscilloscope		
Decade Resistance Box		

Resistors: Two 1 kΩ

One 20 Ω

Capacitors: Two 0.01 μ F

155

13.4   **Procedure:**

A.   Initial Settings of the Oscilloscope:

Set the controls of the oscilloscope to
the following positions:

- Trigger Source & mode to Y_A & Auto.
- (Time/div)   to   50 μ sec.
- (Y - position)   to   center of screen
- (DC - 0 - AC)   to   AC
- (V/div) for Y_A to   0.1V
- (V/div) for Y_B to   2 mV

B.   Characterization of The Source (The CAL-output
of The Oscilloscope):

(1)   Connect (CAL-output) of the oscilloscope
to Y_A. Adjust (Time/div) to display
about one cycle of the source waveform,
V_{Th}. Plot V_{Th} versus time on Graph
13.1.

(2)   Measure the internal resistance, R_{Th} of
the source by connecting the decade
resistance box (R_x) across Y_A. Adjust R_x
until the display is reduced to half of
its initial value. Record V_{Th} and R_{Th} in
Table 13.2. $R_{TH} = 851 \Omega$

Peak to peak.

156

Table 13.2

V_{Th} [V]	R_{Th} [kΩ]
6 dw x 0.1v/div = 0.6v	0.851 k

C.   Transients Measurements:

(1)   Connect the circuit shown in Fig. 13.2;

   R = 1 K Ω   &   C = 0.01 μ F.

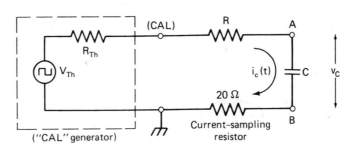

Fig. 13.2

(2)   Connect node (A) to Y_A, and node (B) to Y_B. [The B - trace now displays 20x the current $i_C(t)$, while the A - trace displays (approximately) the voltage $v_C(t)$.] Plot v_C and i_C versus time on Graphs 13.2 and 13.3, respectively.

(3)   Adjust the (Time/div), trigger slope and level controls to measure, as accurately as you can, the charging and discharging time constants [the charging time constant is the amount of time it takes the capacitor's voltage to reach 63% of the voltage step. How about the

Horizon
0.2dw x 50Ms/div
$= 1 \times 10^{-5} s \, \tau$

2.7dw/0.1 = 0.27v
= 0.17v

157

discharging time constant?]   Record your

results in Table 13.3.

(4)   Repeat the above steps for all the

combinations of R & C given in Table

13.1.

3.2 div · 0.1v/div
= 0.32V ⅹ 63℣,
= 0.216V

0.1 div ⅹ 2.4 s/div

= 22 s/s

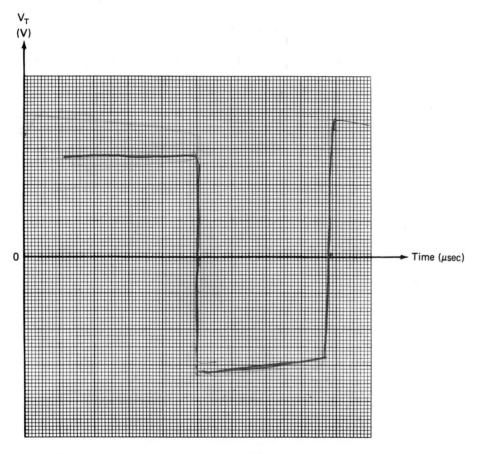

Graph 13.1

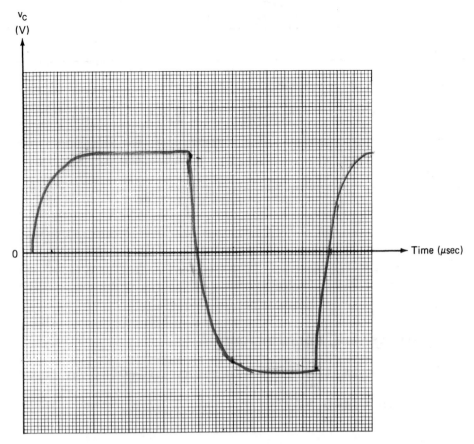

Graph 13.2

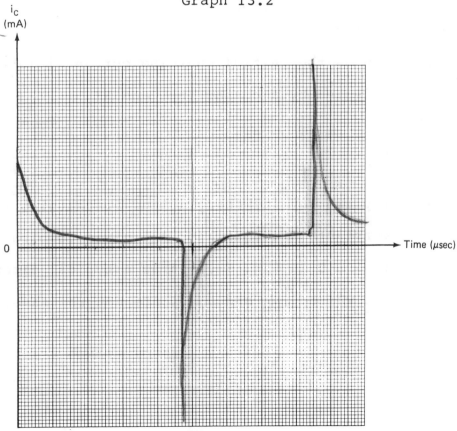

Graph 13.3

159

Table 13.3

C [μF]	$R_T = R_{Th} + R$ [KΩ]	CR_T [μ sec]	τ ch [μ sec]	τ dis [sec]	$i_C(o^+)$ [mA]	
0.01_μ	$= 0.851 + 1$ $= 1.851 K_\Omega$	$18\mu s$ $1.851 \times 10^{-5} s$	$1div \times 20\mu s$ $20\mu sec$	$22\mu sec$	$1.8div \times 5m/div$ $0.45mA$	$= 9mA \div 20$
0.02_μ	$= 1.851 k_\Omega$	$3.7 \times 10^{-5} s$ $37\mu s$	$0.8div \times 50\mu s/div$ $40\mu sec$	$40\mu se$	$0.45mA$	
0.01_μ	$0.851 + 2k_\Omega$ $R_T = 2.851k_\Omega$	2.851×10^{-5} $= 28.5\mu s$	$3.6 \times 10^{-5} sec$ $36\mu sec$	$36\mu se$	$2.6div \times 2m/div$ $= 0.26mA$	$5mA \div 20$

13.5   Comments and Conclusions:

1.   How is the time constant affected by a change in C and R?

2.   How is the initial charging current $i_C(o^+)$ affected by a change in C and R?

3.   Explain why the charging and discharging time constants are equal for any given combination of R & C in Fig. 13.1; draw a typical circuit for which τ ch and τ dis are not the same.

4.   What is the "inherent" error in the procedure
     for displaying v_C versus time?

5.   Comment on your results; do your results
     verify the theoretical expectations? Explain
     the reasons for possible deviations.

14 | TRANSIENTS IN RL-CIRCUITS

<u>Required Reading:</u>   Text, sections 10.3 & 10.4

14.1   **Objective:**

To investigate the transient behaviour of simple RL-circuits.

14.2   **Prelab Assignment:**

Consider the circuit shown in Fig. 14.1. The switch S was in position (a) for a long time and then moved to position (b) at t = o. For each of the combinations of R & L shown in Table 14.1, determine:

(1) the rise and decay time constants,

(2) the size of the current step through the inductor.

163

Table 14.1

Combination #	R [kΩ]	L [mH]
1	2	60
2	2	90
3	1	60

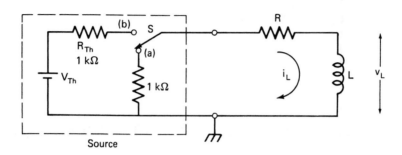

Fig. 14.1

Prelab Work Space:

$$\tau = \frac{L}{R}$$

① $\quad \tau = \frac{60mH}{2k\Omega} = 3 \times 10^{-5} s$

② $\quad \tau = \frac{90mH}{2k\Omega} = 4.5 \times 10^{-5} s$

③ $\quad \tau = \frac{60mH}{1k\Omega} = 6 \times 10^{-5} k\Omega s$

Prelab Work Space:

14.3   **Equipment:**

ITEM	MANUFACTURER AND MODEL NO.	LAB. SERIAL NO
Dual-Beam Oscilloscope		
Decade Inductance Box		

Resistors: Two 1 kΩ

One 20 Ω

14.4   **Procedure:**

A.   **Initial Settings of the Oscilloscope:**

Set the controls of the oscilloscope to the

following positions:

. Trigger Source & mode to Y_A & Auto.

. (Time/div)   to   50 μ sec.

. (DC - O - AC)   to   AC

. (V/div) for Y_A to   O.2V

. (V/div) for Y_B to   2 mV

. (Y - position)   to   center of screen

B.   <u>Transients Measurements</u>:

(1)   Connect the circuit shown in Fig. 14.2;

     R = 2 k Ω &   L = 6O mH

     [V_{Th} and R_{Th} represent the Thevenin's

     equivalent circuit of the (CAL) generator

     of the oscilloscope; See Section 13.4,

     Part B for the values of V_{Th} & R_{Th}.]

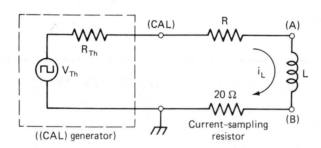

Fig. 14.2

(2)   Connect node (A) to Y_A and node (B) to
     Y_B [the B-trace now displays 20x the
     current $i_L(t)$, while the A-trace
     displays (approximately) the voltage
     $v_L(t)$]. Plot v_L and i_L versus time on
     Graphs 14.1 and 14.2 respectively.

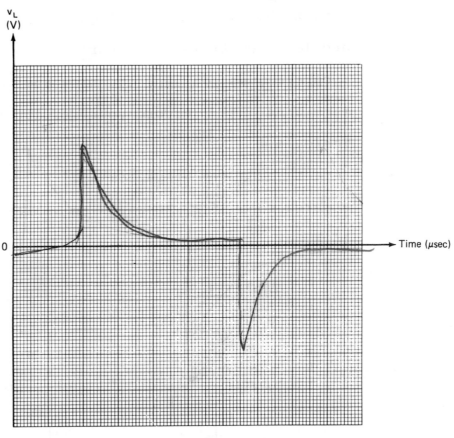

Graph (14.1)

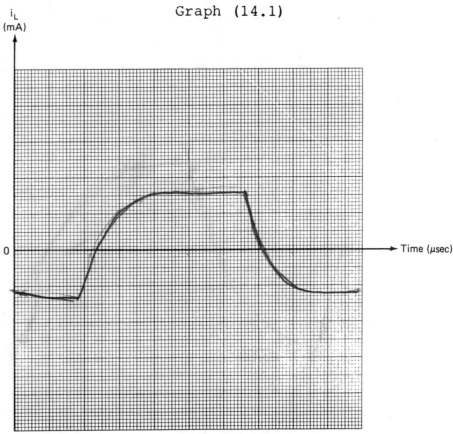

Graph 14.2

167

(3) Adjust the (Time/div), trigger slope
     and level controls to measure, as
     accurately as you can, the rise and decay
     time constants. Record your results in
     Table 14.2.

(4) Repeat the above steps for all
     combinations of R & L given in Table
     14.1.

Table 14.2

$R_{Th} = 0.851 k$ $0.6V$.

L (mH)	$R_T = R_{Th} + R$ [k Ω]	$\dfrac{L}{R_T}$ (μ sec)	τ rise (μ sec)	τ dec (μ sec)	Current Step [mA]
60	2.851				
90	2.851				

14.5   **Comments and Conclusions:**

1.   How is the time constant affected by a change
     in L and R?

2.   How is the final current i_L affected by a
     change in L and R?

3.   How do the waveforms of $v_L(t)$ and $i_L(t)$
      compare to those of $v_C(t)$ and $i_C(t)$ of
      Exp. #13? Explain.

4.   Comment on your results; do your results
      verify the theoretical expectations? Explain
      the reasons for possible deviations.

15 | RESISTIVE AC-CIRCUITS

Required Reading: Text, sections 11.4 & 11.5

15.1   **Objective:**

.   To examine the validity of Kirchhoff's laws for
AC resistive circuits.

.   To **verify the RMS-peak-values relationship** of
sinusoidal waveforms.

15.2   **Prelab Assignment:**

Consider the circuit shown in Fig. 15.1.
$v_T(t)$ is a sinusoidal voltage waveform with a (p-p)
value of 10V @ 200 Hz. Determine the following:

(1)   the RMS value of the voltage of each node
w.r.t. circuit ground, $V_{RMS} = \frac{10}{\sqrt{2}} = 7.07V$

(2)   the RMS value of the current through each
branch,

(3)   the average power dissipated by each element.

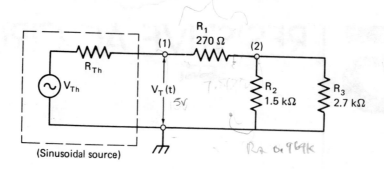

Fig. 15.1 $I\,45mA$ $R_T = 1234.6$

Prelab Work Space:

$V_{peak-peak} = 10V$

$\therefore V_{peak} = 5V$

node 1. $V_① = \dfrac{5v}{\sqrt{2}} = 3.53V$ node 2 $V_② = I \cdot R_②$ $I_2 = \dfrac{V_②}{R_2} = \dfrac{3.856}{1.5k} = 2.57mA$

$I_① = 45mA$ $I_{rms} = 2.82mA$ $= 4mx (964)$ $= 1.81mA\ RMS$

$= 3.856V$

$V_1 = R_1 I_1$ $\div \sqrt{2} = 2.726V$ $I_3 = \dfrac{V_②}{R_3} = \dfrac{3.856}{2.7k} = 1.42mA$

$= \dfrac{1.08v}{\sqrt{2}} = 0.176v$ $= 1mA$

Branch.

$I\ RMS @ ① \rightarrow ②.$

$V_{RMS} = I_{RMS} R$

$I_{RMS} = \dfrac{V_{rms}}{R} = \dfrac{1.08}{270} = 4mA$

15.3   Equipment:

ITEM	MANUFACTURER AND MODEL NO.	LAB. SERIAL NO.
Dual-Beam Oscilloscope		
Signal generator		
DMM or VOM		
Decade Resistance Box		

Resistors: One 10 Ω , 270 Ω , 1.5k Ω & 2.7k Ω

15.4   Procedure:

A.   Verification of Kirchhoff's law for AC Resistive Circuits:

(1)   Connect the circuit shown in Fig. 15.2. Use channel Y_A of the oscilloscope to display the terminal voltage of the signal generator $V_T(t)$.   Adjust V_T (p-p) to 10V @ 200 Hz, while the circuit is connected.

(2)   Use the DMM or the VOM to measure the RMS value of the voltage across the generator's terminals, R_1 and R_2.   Estimate the RMS value of the current through each resistance and record your results in Table 15.1.

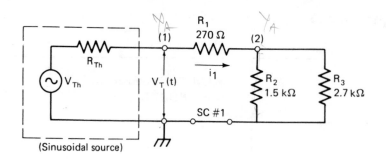

Fig. 15.2

Table 15.1

RMS - Values	Computed	Measured	Units
$V_T = V_1$	3,53.	3,61	✓
V_{R_1}	0,76	0,76	✓
V_{R_2}	2,72	2,82	✓
I_1	2,82 mA	2,91 mA	A
I_2	1,81 mA	1,86 mA	A
I_3	1 mA	1.0 2 mo	A

3.   How does the measured value of V_T compare with
     the sum of the measured values of V_{R_1} and V_{R_2}?

The sum of V_{R_1} and $V_{R_2} = V_T$

174

4.   How does the estimated value of I_1 compare
      with the sum of the estimates of I_2 and I_3?

      The sum of $I_2 + I_3$ is equal
      to the current I_1

B.   Voltage and Current Waveforms for Resistive

      Elements:

      (1)   Use Y_A to display $v_T(t)$; measure the

            peak value of $v_T(t)$.

            V_T (peak) = ...5V..................

            How does V_T (peak) compare with the

            measured RMS value of V_T?

            The peak value of the oscilloscope
            is equal to the RMS value of V_T
            $$V_T = \sqrt{2}\, V_{TRMS}$$

      (2)   Replace SC # 1 with a 10 Ω resistance

            [this is the current-sampling resistance

            that provides a current-to-voltage

            conversion].   Use channel Y_B to display

            the voltage across the 10 Ω resistance.

            Y_B now displays 10 X the current waveform

            $i_1(t)$.   Plot V_T and I_1 versus time on

            Graph 15.1.

175

(3) Estimate the value of $[V_T(t)]^2$ at ten equally-spaced time intervals within half a cycle. Plot your estimates of $[V_T(t)]^2$ versus time, over one cycle, on Graph 15.2. Estimate, roughly, the total area under the curve representing $[V_T(t)]^2$, over one complete cycle.

Area =.....................................

(4) What is the average (mean) value of $[V_T(t)]^2$ over one complete cycle?

Mean $[V_T(t)]^2$ = ...

(5) What is the root-mean-square value of $V_T(t)$?

$\sqrt{\text{Mean } [V_T(t)^2}$ = ...

How does the above result compare with the measure RMS value of V_T?

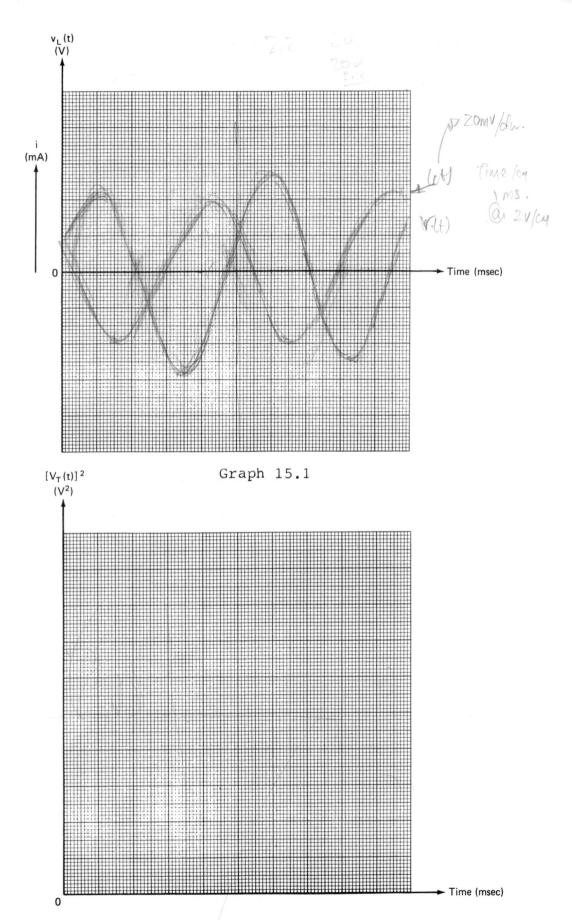

Graph 15.1

Graph 15.2

177

15.5   **Comments and Conclusions:**

1. From Graph 15.1, find the average value of $v_T(t)$ over one cycle.

    Mean $[v_T(t)]$ = ...

2. What is the theoretical ratio of the RMS-to-peak value of a sinusoidal waveform? What would this ratio be for an AC square waveform?

    1 : $\sqrt{2}$ or 1,414.

    No, the ratio between the square wave RMS to peak-p is 1:1

3. Suppose that the sinusoidal source in Fig. 15.2 is replaced by an AC triangular source, would Kirchhoff's laws still apply to your circuit?

    yes, any kind of continuous wave would not affect the current

4. Comment on your results; do the experimental results support the theoretical expectation? Explain the reasons for possible deviations.

    — Calculating the area of the graph was extremely difficult unless calculus is applied to A

16 | SERIES RL-CIRCUITS

Required Reading: Text, section 12.1

16.1   Objective:

- To examine the current-voltage relationship of an inductor for sinusoidal excitation at a constant frequency.

- To examine the current-voltage relationship of a series RL-circuit for sinusoidal excitation with varying frequency.

16.2   Prelab Assignment:

(1) Given a 0.5 H coil with unknown internal resistance r_L; its impedance triangle at 5 kHz has a phase angle of 84°. Determine r_L and the ratio of X_L to r_L at 5 kHz.

(2) A sinusoidal source and a 15 k Ω resistance are added in series with the above coil as shown in Fig. 16.1. The terminal voltage of

the source is maintained at 10V p-p, while
the frequency is adjusted to each of the
following values:

0.5, 1, 2, 5, 10 and 15 kHz.

a. Determine I (p-p) and the phase
angle ($\phi°$) of V_T (w.r.t. I) for each of
the above frequency values; calculate the
magnitude of the input impedance $\left|Z_{in}\right|$ in
each case.

b. Use Graphs 16.1 & 16.2 to plot $\left|Z_{in}\right|$
and ($\phi°$) versus frequency, respectively.

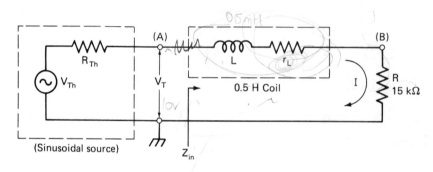

Fig. 16.1

Prelab Work Space:

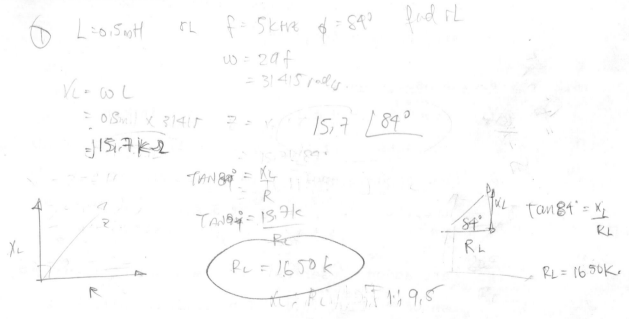

180

Prelab Work Space:

Frequency	0.15kHz	1kHz	2kHz	10kHz	15kHz	5kHz
ω rad/s	3141.59	6283.18	12566	62831.8	94247	
$jX_L \ \Omega$	1.57k	3.14k	6.28k	31.41k	47.12k	jKL 15.7k
$r_L \ \Omega$	1.65k	1.65k	1.65k	1.65k	1.65k	1.65
ϕ	43.7°	64.42°	75.36°	87.01°	89.93°	89°
Z_{in}	2.27 $\angle$43.7°	3.54 $\angle$64.42°	6.49 $\angle$75.36°	31.45 $\angle$87.01°	4A.14 $\angle$28.73°	
Z_T	16.65 $+j$1.57	16.65 j 3.14	16.65 j 6.28			
$=$	16.57 $\angle$5.38°	16.94 $\angle$10.67°	17.79 $\angle$20.16°	35.5 $\angle$62°	45.29 $\angle$70.53°	

$R = 15k\Omega$

$$I = \frac{C}{Z_T} = 3.53 \angle$$

$$Z_T = r_L + R + JX_L$$

16.65k $+j$1.57

16.75 $\angle$5.377°

So for 0.15kHz.

i.e. then $JX_L = \omega L$

$$= 2\pi (0.15)(0.15)$$
$$= j1.57k\Omega$$

$$Z_T = (R_L + R_{in}) + j1.57k$$
$$= (1.65k + 15k) + j1.57$$
$$= 16.72 \angle 5.38°$$

181

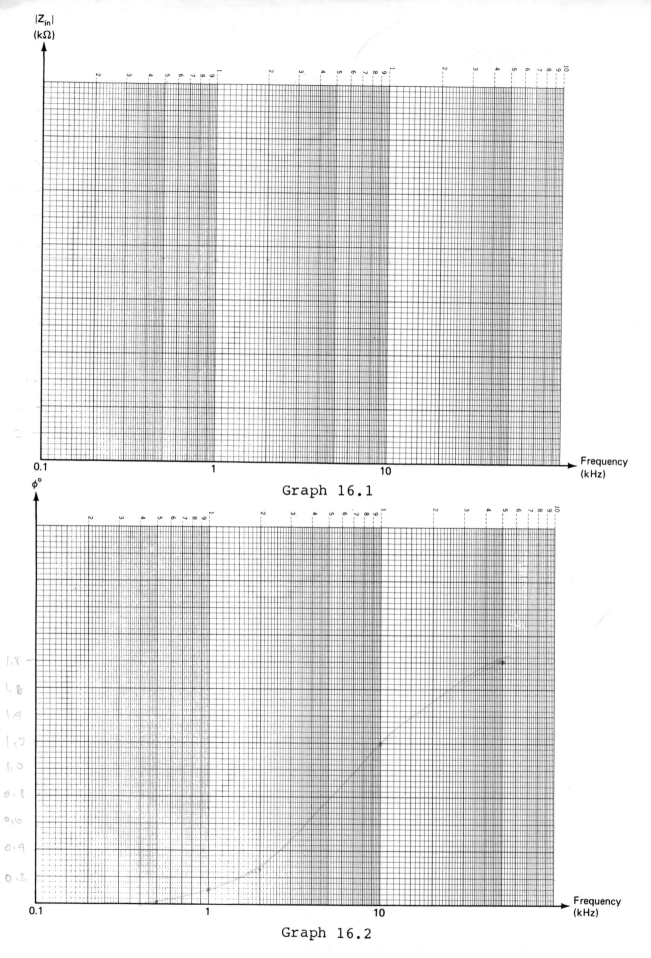

Graph 16.1

Graph 16.2

182

16.3   Equipment:

ITEM	MANUFACTURER AND MODEL NO.	LAB. SERIAL NO.
Dual-Beam Oscilloscope		
Signal Generator		
Decade Inductance Box		

Resistors: One   10 Ω & 15 k Ω

16.4 Procedure:

A.   The I-V Relationship of an Inductor for Sinusoidal Excitation:

(1)   Connect the circuit shown in Fig. 16.2.   Use channel Y_A of the oscilloscope to display V_T; adjust V_T (p-p) to 10V at 5 kHz.

(2)   Use channel Y_B to display the voltage across the 20Ω resistor [V/div @ 2mV]. Y_B now displays 20 X the current I, while Y_A displays (approximately) the voltage across the coil.   Use Graph 16.3 to plot one cycle of both displays versus time.

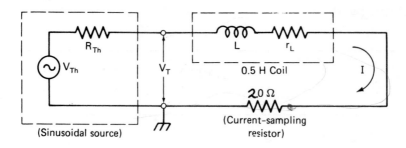

Fig. 16.2

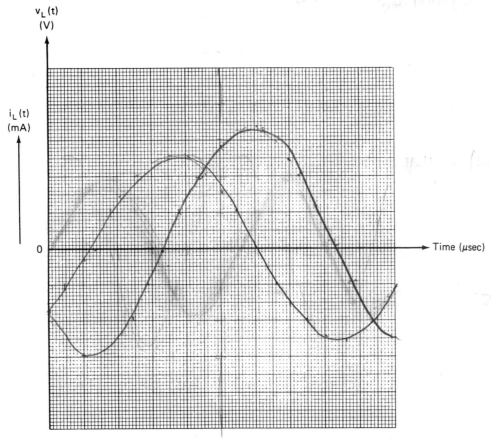

Graph 16.3

(3) Use Graph 16.4 to plot the phasor
diagram (V & I) for the coil at 5 kHz;
estimate the value of r_L and the ratio of
X_L to r_L at 5 kHz.

r_L = ...

X_L/r_L = ...

Graph 16.4

B. Frequency Response of Simple RL-Circuit:

(1) Connect the circuit shown in Fig. 16.1.
Use Y_A to display V_T and Y_B to display
the voltage of node (B) w.r.t. ground [Y_B
now displays 15 k X I].

(2) Adjust V_T (p-p) to 10V at 5 kHz.
Measure I (p-p) and the phase angle ($\phi°$)
of V_T (w.r.t. I). [See Section 16.6,
Appendix A: Phase Measurement.]
Calculate the magnitude of the input
impedance Z_{in}, and record in Table
16.1.

185

(3) Repeat step #2 for all the frequency

settings shown in Table 16.1.

Table 16.1

Frequency (kHz)	0.5	1	2	5	10	15
I (p-p) (mA)	16.8V/15k 1.12mA	8A/15k 0.56mA	8.6/15k 0.573mA	7.2v/15k 0.48mA	5/15k 0.2mA	2/15k 0.133mA
$\lvert Z_{in} \rvert$ (kΩ)						
(φ°) (degrees)	5.65˙	11.2	30°	58.69° -43.3	75°	90° 90,

(3) Plot $\lvert Z_{in} \rvert$ and (φ°) versus frequency on

Graphs 16.1 & 16.2, respectively.

16.5   **Comments and Conclusions:**

1. How is the phase angle (φ°) affected by:

(a) a change in frequency,

(b) a change in inductance,

or (c) a change in resistance?

2. How is the magnitude of the input impedance
$\lvert Z_{in} \rvert$ affected by:

(a)   a change in frequency,

(b)   a change in inductance,

or   (c)   a change in resistance?

3.   Comment on your results; do your results
      agree with the theoretical expectations?
      Explain the reasons for possible deviations.

16.6   Appendix A: Phase Measurement

The following procedure is recommended for
measuring the phase angle between two sinusoidal
signals displayed by a dual-beam oscilloscope.

1.   Set the controls of the oscilloscope to the
      following positions:

      .Trigger Source, mode & slope to Y_A, Auto & ($^+$).

      .(Y - position)   to   center of screen

      .(DC - 0 - AC)   to   (AC)

2.   Apply one sinusoid to Y_A and the other
      sinusoid to Y_B. Adjust both (V/div) such that

187

the (p-p) values of both sinusoids extend over the full height of the screen.

3. Adjust (Time/div) & (trigger slope and level) to set the display of <u>one-half cycle</u> of the Y_A-sinusoid to precisely <u>nine horizontal divisions</u>. [Each division now represents 20 degrees.]

4. Measure the phase angle ($\phi°$) <u>of the Y_A-display w.r.t. the Y_B-display</u> as:

    $\phi°$ [leading] = [No. of horizontal divisions between the positive zero-crossings of both displays] X $20°$, as shown in Fig. 16.3a.

    $\phi°$ [lagging] = [No. of horizontal divisions between the negative zero-crossings of both displays] X $20°$, as shown in Fig. 16.3b.

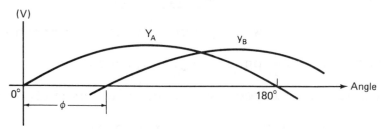

Fig. 16.3a

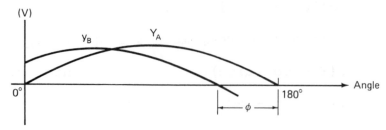

Fig. 16.3b

188

17 | SERIES RC-CIRCUITS

$$\frac{2,4}{0,6} = \frac{180°}{x}$$

$$x = 45°$$

17.1   Objective:

-   To examine the current-voltage relationship of
    a capacitor for sinusoidal excitation at a
    constant frequency.

-   To examine the current-voltage relationship of
    a series RC-circuit for sinusoidal excitation
    with varying frequency.

17.2   Prelab Assignment:

Consider the circuit shown in Fig. 17.1.
The terminal voltage of the source is maintained at
10V p-p, while the frequency is adjusted to each of
the following values:

    0.5, 1, 2, 5, 10 and 15 kHz.

a. Determine I (p-p) and the phase angle ($\phi°$)
    of V_T (w.r.t. I) for each of the above

189

frequency values; calculate the magnitude

of the input impedance $|Z_{in}|$ in each case.

b. Use Graphs 17.1 & 17.2 to plot $|Z_{in}|$

and ($\phi°$) versus frequency, respectively.

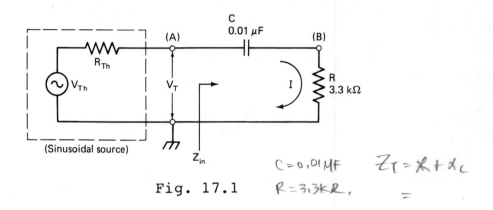

Fig. 17.1

$C = 0.01 \mu F$ $Z_T = \mathcal{R} + \chi_c$

$R = 3.3 k \mathcal{R}$, $=$

$f = 0.15, 1, 2, 5 \quad 10 \, kHz$

Prelab Work Space:

$V_T = 10v \, pp$

$= 5 v p$

$= 3.53 V_{RMS}$

Prelab Work Space:

Frequency   0.5   1   2   5   10   15   kHz

$X_c = \dfrac{1}{2\pi f C}$ 31.8k   15.915k   7.957k   3.183k   1.591k   1.061 K

$= 3.3K\Omega$,   32 $\angle -84$ 16.12 $\angle -78$ 8.16 $\angle -67.47$ 4.5 $\angle -43.9$ 3.66 $\angle -25.7$ 3.46 $\angle -17.8$

$Z_{in} =$

$R + X_c$

$E \; 3.53 \angle 0°$ $I = \dfrac{3.53}{3.66 \angle -25.7}$

                              0.96 A

        3.3 $\sqrt{10}$

                   3336

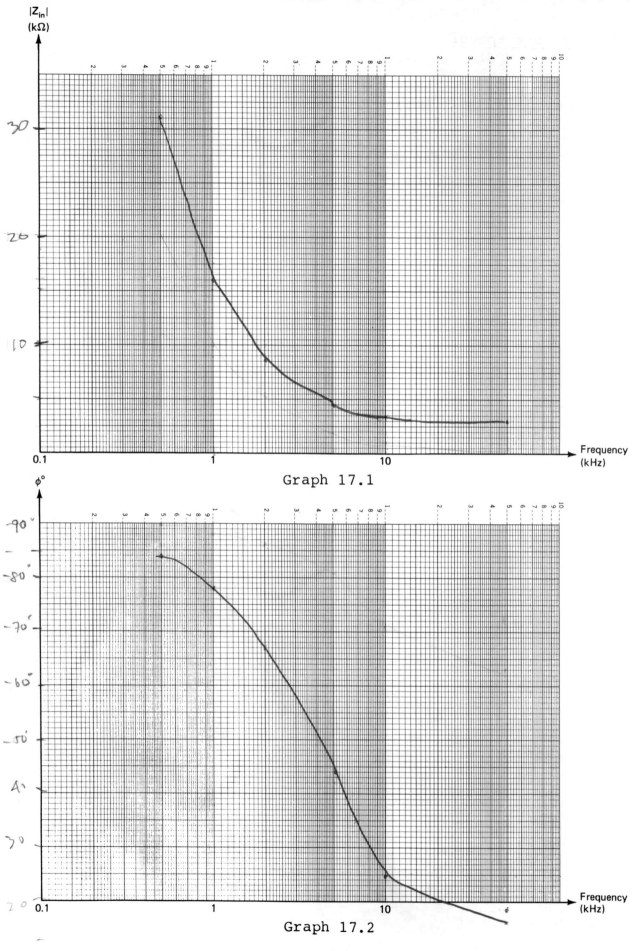

Graph 17.1

Graph 17.2

17.3   **Equipment:**

ITEM	MANUFACTURER AND MODEL NO.	LAB. SERIAL NO
Dual-Beam Oscilloscope		
Signal Generator		

Capacitors: One $0.01\,\mu F$

Resistors: One $10\,\Omega$ & $3.3\ k\Omega$

17.4   **Procedure:**

A.   The I-V Relationship of a Capacitor for
     Sinusoidal Excitation:

   (1)   Connect the circuit shown in Fig. 17.2.
         Use channel Y_A of the oscilloscope to
         display V_T; adjust V_T (p-p) to 10V at
         5 kHz.

   (2)   Use channel Y_B to display the voltage
         across the $10\,\Omega$ resistor [V/div @ 5 mV].
         Y_B now displays 10 X the current I, while
         Y_A displays (approximately) the voltage
         across the capacitor. Use Graph 17.3
         to plot one cycle of both displays versus
         time.

  (3)   Use Graph 17.4 to plot the phasor
         diagram (V & I) for the capacitor at
         5 kHz.

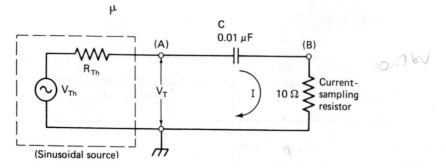

μ

C
0.01 μF

(A)   (B)

R_{Th}

V_{Th} V_T I   10 Ω   Current-sampling resistor

(Sinusoidal source)

Fig. 17.2

0.76V

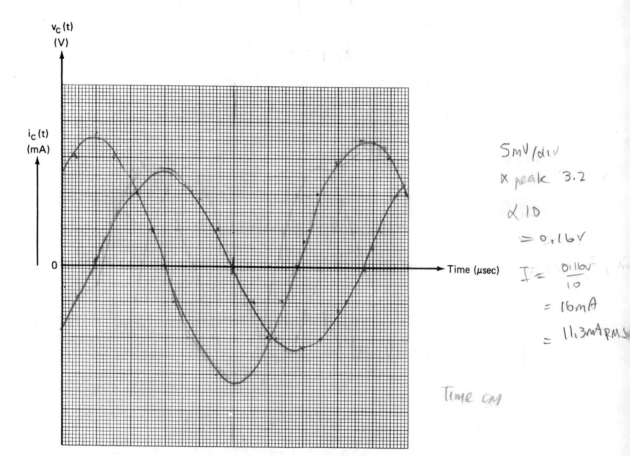

$v_C(t)$
(V)

$i_C(t)$
(mA)

0

Time (μsec)

Graph 17.3

5mV/div
x peak 3.2
× 10
= 0.16V

$I = \dfrac{0.16V}{10}$

= 16mA

= 11.3mA RMS

Time cm

$\dfrac{180}{4.25} \times 2.2 = \emptyset 93.17°$

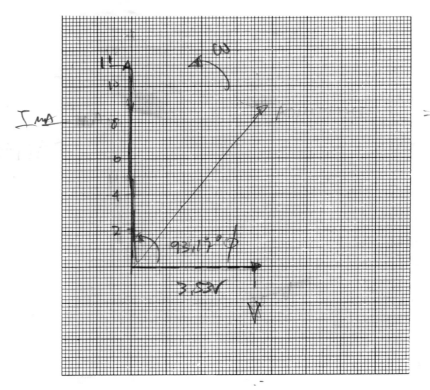

Graph 17.4

B. Frequency Response of Simple RC-Circuit:

  (1)   Connect the circuit shown in Fig. 17.1.
Use Y_A to display V_T and Y_B to display
the voltage of node (B) w.r.t. ground [Y_B
now displays 3.3 k X I].

  (2)   Adjust V_T (p-p) to 10V at 5 kHz.
Measure I (p-p) and the phase angle ($\phi°$)
of V_T (w.r.t. I) [See Section 16.6.]
Calculate the magnitude of the input
impedance $\left|Z_{in}\right|$, and record in Table
17.1.

  (3)   Repeat step #2 for all the frequency
settings shown in Table 17.1.

  (4)   Plot $\left|Z_{in}\right|$ and ($\phi°$) versus frequency on
Graphs 17.1 & 17.2, respectively.

Table 17.1

Frequency (kHz)	0.5	1	2	5	10	15	
I (p-p) (mA)	1.12/9.9k 0.90mA	2.5/9.9k 0.175mA	4.2/3.3k 1.27mA	7m/3.3k 2.12mA	10/3.3 4.84mA	16A/3.3 4.90mA	$\frac{180}{DIV} \times \phi = \phi$
$\lvert Z_{in}\rvert$ (kΩ) $R+X_C$	32∠-84°	16.2∠-78	8.6∠67.5	4.5∠44°	3.66∠-25.7	3.46∠-17.6	
($\phi°$) (degrees)	-90°	-81°	-67.76°	-41.08°	-26.25°	-17.68°	

17.5   Comments and Conclusions:

1.   How is the phase angle ($\phi°$) affected by:

(a)   a change in frequency,

(b)   a change in resistance,

or   (c)   a change in capacitance?

a) as the frequency changes, the phase angle changes, however it does not change proportionally.

b) a change in resistance cause a decrease in phase angle in the circuit

c)

2.   How is the magnitude of the input impedance

$|z_{in}|$ affected by:

   (a)   a change in frequency,

   (b)   a change in resistance,

or   (c)   a change in capacitance?

a) By changing the frequency, the impedance increases.

b) changing to a smaller resistance the impedance increases slightly.

3.   Comment on your results; do your results agree with the theoretical expectations? Explain the reasons for possible deviations.

$$T = \frac{1}{f} = 2 \times 10^{-9} s.$$

$$\frac{2 \times 10^{-7}}{20 \Omega} = 10 \, d \, \omega.$$

18 | SERIES R-L-C CIRCUITS

Required Reading: Text, sections 12.3 and 14.1

18.1   **Objective:**

To examine the current-voltage relationship of a series R-L-C circuit for sinusoidal excitation at a varying frequency.

18.2   **Prelab Assignment:**

Consider the circuit shown in Fig. 18.1. The 0.5 H coil has an r_L of 1 kΩ at 2.25 kHz. The terminal voltage of the sinusoidal source is maintained at 10V (p-p), while the frequency is varied over the range: $0 < f < \infty$.

(1)   Determine the frequency at which the magnitude of the current I is maximum.

(2)   Determine the frequency at which the phase angle ($\phi°$) of V_T (w.r.t.I) is:

$0°$, $+45°$ and $-45°$

(3) Determine V_C (p-p) at resonance.

(4) Draw the phasor diagram [I, V_T, V_L and V_{r_L}]

   at: 2 kHz, 2.25 kHz and 2.5 kHz.

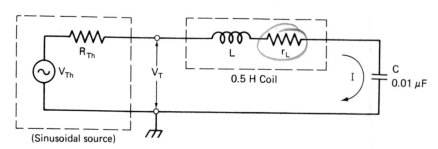

(Sinusoidal source)

Fig. 18.1

Prelab Work Space: $R_L = 1k$ @ $2.25kHz$, $E = 10vpp$.

1. @ maximum current "I" = resonance.

   $\therefore$ $X_L = X_C$ $\therefore$ $\omega L = \dfrac{1}{\omega C}$ $\omega = \dfrac{1}{\sqrt{0.5(0.01M)}}$

   $\omega^2 = \dfrac{1}{LC}$

   $\omega = \dfrac{1}{\sqrt{LC}}$ $= 14142.13 \, rads/sec.$

   $\omega = 2\pi f$ $f = \dfrac{\omega}{2\pi} = 2.25 \, kHz.$

2. frequency at which $\phi = 0°$
   occurs at resonance = $2.25 \, kHz.$

   $\phi = 45°$ $2X_L = X_C$ $\phi = -45°$ $X_L = 2X_C$

   $2\omega L = \dfrac{1}{\omega C}$ $\omega L = \dfrac{2}{\omega C}$

   $\omega^2 = \dfrac{1}{2LC}$ $\omega^2 = \dfrac{2}{LC}$

   $\omega = \dfrac{1}{\sqrt{2LC}}$ $\omega = \dfrac{\sqrt{2}}{\sqrt{LC}}$

   $= 10000 rad$ $f = 20000 rad$

   $= 1.59 \, kHz.$ $f = 3.188 \, kHz.$

200

At resonance

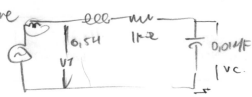

$f = 2.25\,kn. = 14137.11$

$$Z_T = r_L + j(X_L - X_c)$$
$$= 1000 + j(0)$$
$$Z_T = 1000\,\Omega$$
$$Z_T = 1000\,\angle 0°$$

$$V_L = X_L \cdot I$$
$$=$$

$E = 10 Vpp$
$= 5 Vp$
$= 3.53 V\,rms.$
$= 3.53 \angle 0°$

$$I_T = \frac{E}{Z_T} = \frac{3.53 \angle 0°}{1000 \angle 0°}$$
$$= 3.533\,mA\,\angle 0°.$$

$$X_c = \frac{1}{wc} = \frac{1}{(0.01)(14137.11)}$$
$$= 7073.55\,\Omega$$

$$V_c = I \cdot X_c = 25 V$$

$$Vpp = 25 \times 2 \times \sqrt{2}$$
$$= 70.7 V.$$

@ 2.25 knz

$$\uparrow R \rightarrow$$
$$I \quad V_R = 1000 \cdot (3.53) \angle 0°$$
$$= 3535 V$$

@ 2.5 km

$X_L = 7853.98\,\Omega$
$X_c = 6366.19\,\Omega$
$$Z_T = R + j(X_L - X_c)$$
$$= 1000 + j(1487.79)$$
$$= 1792.6 \angle 56.1°$$
$$I = \frac{E}{R} = 1.96\,mA \angle 56.1°$$

$V_L = I X_L = 15.39$
$V_c = I X_c = 12.47$
$V_R = I R = 1.96 V$

@ 2 knz. $W = 12566.37\,rad/se$,

$$X_L = wL$$
$$= (12566.37)(0.15)$$
$$= 6283.18.5\,\Omega$$

$$X_c = \frac{1}{wc} = 7957.74\,\Omega$$

$$Z_T = R + j(X_L - X_c)$$
$$= 1000 + j(-1679.55)$$
$$= 1950 \angle -59.15°$$

$$I = \frac{E}{Z_T} = \frac{3.53 \angle 0°}{1950 \angle -59.15} = 1.8 \angle 59.15\,mA.$$

$V_L = I X_c = 11.3 \angle 59.5°$
$V_c = I X_c = 14.32 \angle 59.15°$
$V_R = I \cdot R = 1.8 \angle 59.15 \angle -00 0$
$= 1.8 \angle 59.15 V.$

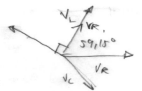

ITEM	MANUFACTURER AND MODEL NO.	LAB. SERIAL NO
Dual-Beam Oscilloscope		
Signal generator		
Decade Inductance Box		

Resistors: One 10 Ω

Capacitors: Two 0.01 μ F

18.4   Procedure:

(1)   Connect the circuit shown in Fig. 18.2.
      Use channel Y_A of the oscilloscope to
      display V_T; adjust V_T (p-p) to 10V at
      any frequency (range 0.5 -- 10 kHz).

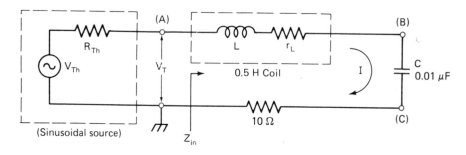

Fig. 18.2

(2)   Use Y_B to display the voltage across the 10 Ω
      resistor. Y_B now displays 10 X I. Adjust the
      frequency of the signal generator until $|I|$
      reaches its maximum value; this frequency is
      now referred to as "f_r". Measure I (p-p) and
      $= 2500$ Hz
      the phase angle ($\phi°$) of V_T w.r.t. I [See

Section 16.6]. Calculate the magnitude of the
input impedance $|Z_{in}|$, and record your
results in Table 18.1.

(3) Connect Y_B to display the voltage of node (B).
Y_B now displays (approximately) the voltage
across the capacitor V_C. Measure V_C (p-p).
Calculate the magnitude of X_C and record in
Table 18.1.

Table 18.1

Frequency	Hz	I (p-p) (mA)	$\|Z_{in}\|$ (kΩ)	$\phi°$ (°)	V_C (p-p) (V)	X_C (kΩ)
$0.2f_r$	500					
$0.5f_r$						
$0.8f_r$						
$0.9f_r$						
f_r	2800Hz	V=0,072V 7.2mA	0.96k	0	12V	7.17k
$1.1f_r$						
$1.2f_r$						
$2f_r$	5000	8mV $I_{PP}=0.8mA$				
$5f_r$	1215k					

(4) Connect Y_B again to display 10 X I and repeat
the above set of measurements for all the

203

Z_{in}

frequency settings shown in Table 18.1.

(5) Plot Z_{in} and ($\phi°$) versus frequency on Graphs 18.1 and 18.2, respectively

(6) Plot the ratio of $V_C(p-p)/V_T(p-p)$ versus frequency on Graph 18.3.

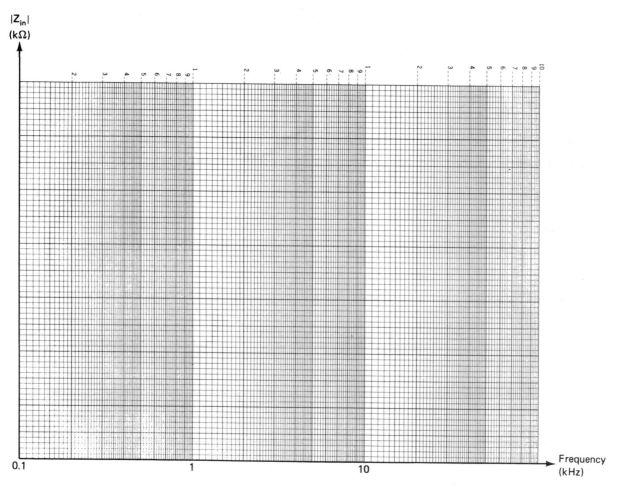

Graph 18.1

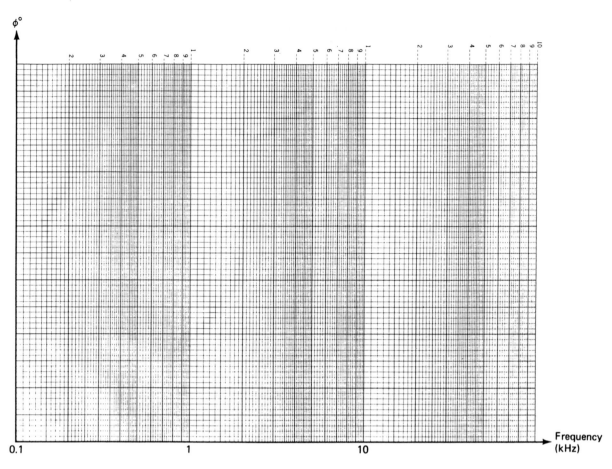

Graph 18.2

(7) Set the decade inductance box to 0.6 H. With Y_A displaying V_T and Y_B displaying 10 X I adjust the frequency of the signal generator until the circuit resonates; record f_r in Table 18.2.

(8) Repeat Step # 7 for:

(a) $L = 0.4\ H$ & $C = 0.01\ \mu F$

(b) $L = 0.5\ H$ & $C = 0.02\ \mu F$

(c) $L = 0.5\ H$ & $C = 0.005\ \mu F$

Table 18.2

L (H)	C (μF)	f_r (kHz)
0.5	0.01	2.72kHz
0.6	0.01	2.040kHz
0.4	0.01	2.569kHz
0.5	0.02	1.587kHz
0.5	0.005	3.125kHz

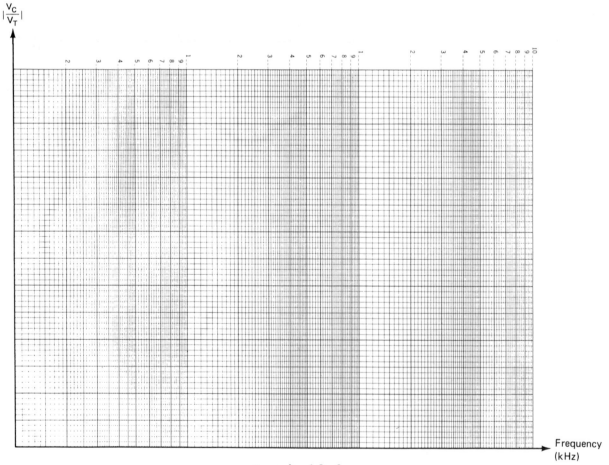

Graph 18.3

<u>Comments and Conclusions:</u>

1. Use Table 18.1 to determine the value of X_C, X_L and r_L at resonance.

2. How are the magnitude and phase of Z_{in} affected by the change in frequency?

3. Note that V_C at f_r is greater than the total applied voltage V_T. Does this mean that Kirchhoff's voltage law does not apply for series resonant circuits? Explain briefly.

4.	How is f_r affected by a change in:

	(a)	L,

or	(b)	C?

5.	Comment on your results; do your results support the theoretical expectations? Explain the reasons for possible deviations.

19 | PARALLEL R-L-C CIRCUITS

Required Reading: Text, sections 12.4, 14.2 and 14.3

19.1   Objective:

To examine the voltage-current relationship of a parallel R-L-C circuit for sinusoidal excitation with varying frequency.

19.2   Prelab Assignment:

A.. Consider the circuit shown in Fig. 19.1. The 5 mH coil has an internal resistance of r_L of 25 Ω at 2.25 kHz. Determine:

(1) the frequency at which Z_{in} is real (other than O Hz).

(2) the frequency at which Z_{in} is maximum.

(3) the frequency at which $X_L = X_C$.

B. Repeat Part A when an additional resistance of 20 Ω is connected in series with the coil-section of the circuit.

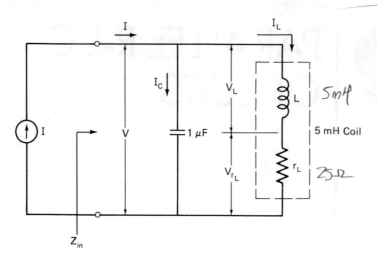

Fig. 19.1

C. Draw the phasor diagram for all the voltages and current in Fig. 19.1 at the frequency where Z_{in} is real.

Prelab Work Space:

$\omega = 2.25 \, kHz \, ?$

$$\omega_0 = \sqrt{\frac{1}{LC} - \left(\frac{R}{L}\right)^2} = 13,22r \text{ rads}.$$

when
$X_L = X_C$

$$\omega = \frac{1}{\sqrt{LC}} = \frac{1}{\sqrt{5m(1m)}} \, \text{?} \, 14142.13 \text{ rads}$$

at 20Ω, r_L.

$$\omega_0 = \sqrt{\frac{1}{5m(1m)} - \left(\frac{20}{5m}\right)^2}$$

$$= \sqrt{2 \times 10^8 - 1.6 \times 10^7}$$

$$= 13564 \text{ rad/s}.$$

210

<u>Prelab Work Space:</u>

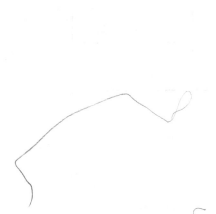

19.3　Equipment:

ITEM	MANUFACTURER AND MODEL NO.	LAB. SERIAL NO
Dual-Beam Oscilloscope		
Signal Generator		
Decade Inductance Box		

Resistors:　One 20 Ω &　10 kΩ

Capacitors:　One 1 μ F

19.4　Procedure:

(1)　Connect the circuit shown in Fig. 19.2.
Use channel Y_A of the oscilloscope to
display V_T; adjust V_T (p-p) to 10V at
any frequency (range 1 -- 10 kHz).
[Note that since $|Z_{in}| \ll 10$ kΩ , I is
approximately constant (independent of
frequency).

$$I \ (\text{p-p}) \ = \ \frac{10}{(10k + Z_{in})} \ \approx \ \frac{10}{10k} \ = 1 \ \text{mA}$$

[Thus, Y_A displays 10k x I]

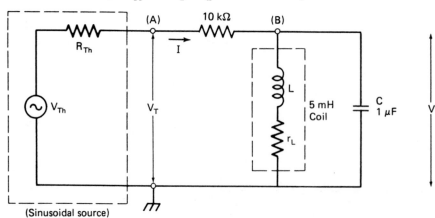

(Sinusoidal source)

Fig. 19.2

212

Connect Y_B to display the voltage of node (B). Y_B now displays the voltage V across the parallel tuned circuit. Adjust the frequency of the signal generator until I & V displays are in phase; this frequency is now referred to as f_o. Measure V (p-p) and determine $|Z_{in}|$.

(3) Adjust the frequency to each of the settings shown in Table 19.1; measure V (p-p) and the phase angle of V w.r.t. I. Calculate $|Z_{in}|$ and record your results.

Table 19.1

Frequency	(Hz)	V(p-p) (mV)	$|Z_{in}|$ (Ω)	ϕ° (°)
0.1f_o	202	24	24	19,6
0.5f_o	1010	48	48	39,3
0.8f_o	1616	110	110	40.
0.9f_o	1818	156	156	27,2
f_o	2020	200	200	0°
1.1f_o	2222	195	195	26,2°
1.2f_o	2929	180	180	39,5
2f_o	4040 20200	44	44	81,8
10f_o		8	8	29,5

(4) Adjust the frequency (on both sides of f_o) until Z_{in} drops to $0.707\ Z_{in}$ max. The frequency difference between these two frequencies is referred to as the frequency bandwidth (BW) of the tuned circuit.

BW = ...

The ratio (f_o/BW) is a measure of the frequency selectivity of the tuned circuit; is known as the quality factor (Q).

Q = ...

(5) Plot Z_{in} and ($\phi°$) versus frequency on Graphs 19.1 & 19.2, respectively.

(6) Add a 20 Ω resistance in series with the coil-section of the circuit shown in Fig. 19.2. Repeat all the above measurements and record in Table 19.2.

BW = ...

Q = ...

Table 19.2

Frequency	(Hz)	V(p-p) (mV)	$\lvert Z_{in}\rvert$ (Ω)	$\phi°$ (°)
$0.1f_o$				
$0.5f_o$				
$0.8f_o$				
$0.9f_o$				
f_o				
$1.1f_o$				
$1.2f_o$				
$2f_o$				
$10f_o$				

(7)   Plot Z_{in} and ($\phi°$) versus frequency on

Graphs 19.1 & 19.2, respectively.

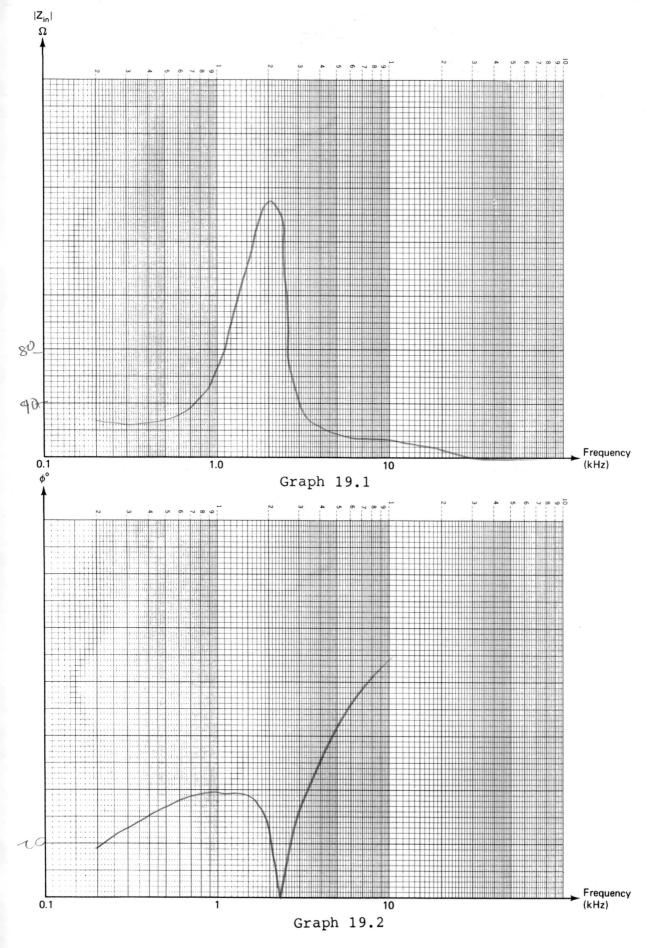

Graph 19.1

Graph 19.2

216

19.5   **Comments and Conclusions:**

1.   How are the magnitude and phase of Z_{in}
      affected by the change in frequency?

2.   How is f_o affected by:

      (a)   a change in L or C,

      (b)   adding extra resistance in series with
            the coil section?

3.   How are the quality factor and bandwidth
      affected by the addition of the $20\,\Omega$
      resistor?

4. Comment on your results; do your results support the theoretical expectations? Explain the reasons for possible deviations.

20 | SIMPLE FILTER CIRCUITS

Required Reading: Text, section 12.2

20.1   Objective:

To examine the frequency response (magnitude and phase) of simple low-pass and high-pass filters.

20.2   Prelab Assignment:

Consider the circuits shown in Fig. 20.1. The terminal voltage of the sinusoidal source is maintained at **2** V (p-p), while the frequency is varied.

For each circuit, determine the following:

a. the ratio of V_O/V_T as a function of ω (rad/sec).

$X_c = 0,01\mu F$

$$E = 0,707V . = V_T \qquad Z_T = \sqrt{R^2 + \left(\tfrac{1}{\omega c}\right)^2} \qquad X = \tfrac{1}{\omega c}$$

$$V_6 = \frac{E}{Z_T} \cdot X_c$$

$$\frac{V_\delta}{V_T} = \frac{E X_c}{Z_T} = \frac{X_c}{Z_T}$$
$$E$$

219

b.   the magnitude of V_o/V_T at

   $\omega = 0$ & $\omega = \infty$

c.   the magnitude and phase of V_o/V_T at

   $\omega = 1/CR$ rad/sec.

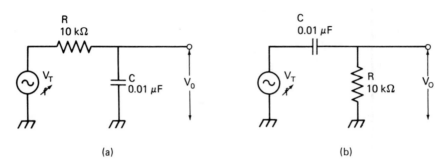

(a)   (b)

Fig. 20.1

Prelab Work Space:

a) $\dfrac{V_o}{V_T} = \dfrac{X_c}{Z_T} = \dfrac{\frac{1}{wc}}{\sqrt{R^2 + (\frac{1}{wc})^2}}$

$= \dfrac{1}{wc\sqrt{R^2 + (\frac{1}{wc})^2}}$

at $w=0$

$\boxed{\dfrac{V_o}{V_T} = \dfrac{X_c}{Z_T} = \dfrac{|Z_T|}{|Z_T|} = 1}$

$\dfrac{V_o}{V_T} = \dfrac{0}{\sqrt{|Z_T| + 0}}$

$= 0$

b) at $w=0$ then $\phi = -90'$

$R = |Z_T|\cos\theta \qquad = R = |Z_T|\cos(-90) = 0$

$X_c = -|Z_T|\sin\phi \qquad X_c = -|Z_T|\sin(-90)$

$\qquad\qquad\qquad\qquad = |Z_T|$

at $w = \alpha$.

then $\phi = 0'$ $R = |Z_T|$

$\qquad\qquad X_c = 0$

$\therefore$ at $w = \alpha$

then $\dfrac{V_o}{V_T} = 0$

220

Prelab Work Space:

Equipment:

ITEM	MANUFACTURER AND MODEL NO.	LAB. SERIAL NO.
Dual-Beam Oscilloscope		
Signal Generator		

Resistors: One 10 k Ω

Capacitors: One 0.01 μF

20.4   **Procedure:**

A.   The Frequency Response of a Simple Low-Pass
Filter

(1)   Connect the circuit shown in Fig. 20.2. Use
channel Y_A of the oscilloscope to display
V_T; adjust V_T (p-p) to 2 V at 100 Hz.

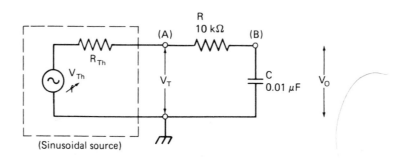

Fig. 20.2

(2)   Connect Y_B to display V_O. Measure
V_O (p-p) and the phase angle ($\phi°$) of V_O
w.r.t. V_T (See Section 16.6). Determine
the ratio of V_O (p-p)/V_T (p-p) and
record your results in Table 20.1.

(3) Repeat the above set of measurements for all
     the frequency settings shown in Table 20.1.

6

Table 20.1

Frequency (Hz)	100	500	1000	2000	5000	10,000
$\dfrac{V_O(p\text{-}p)}{V_T(p\text{-}p)}$ (V/V)	$\dfrac{2}{2}=1$	$\dfrac{1.75}{2}$ 0.875	$\dfrac{1.6}{2}$ 0.80	$\dfrac{1.12}{1.9}$ -0.59	$\dfrac{0.56}{1.9}$ 0.29	$\dfrac{0.28}{1.9}$ 0.147
$\phi°$ (degrees)	0	18°	36.6°	50.9°	67.5 / 72°	79.2°

(4) Plot V_O/V_T and ($\phi°$) versus frequency on Graphs 20.1
     & 20.2, respectively.

     Determine the frequency (f_O) at which $V_O/V_T = 0.707$.

B.   <u>The Frequency Response of a Simple High-Pass Filter</u>

(1) Interchange R and C in the circuit shown in Fig.
     20.2.

(2) Repeat as in Part (A) and record your results in
     Table 20.2.

223

Table 20.2

Frequency (Hz)	100	500	1000	2000	5000	10,000
$\dfrac{V_O \text{ (p-p)}}{V_T \text{ (p-p)}}$ (V/V)	$\dfrac{01108}{2} = 0.06$ 0.054	$\dfrac{016}{195}$ 0.307	$\dfrac{1.104}{119}$ 0.547	$\dfrac{1.96}{1.9}$ 0.768	$\dfrac{1.75}{1.875}$	$\dfrac{1.8}{1.875}$ 0.19p
$\phi°$ (degrees)	86.9	67.3 72°	-66° 59°	45° 36°	25.7 14.9	6.4° 10.8

V_B is leading

(3) Plot V_O/V_T and ($\phi°$) versus frequency on

Graphs 20.1 & 20.2, respectively.

Determine the frequency (f_O) at which

$$\left| V_O/V_T \right| = 0.707$$

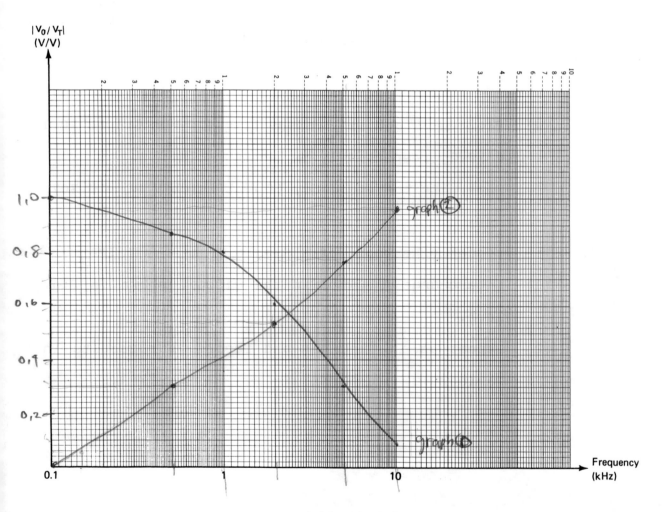

Graph 20.1

224

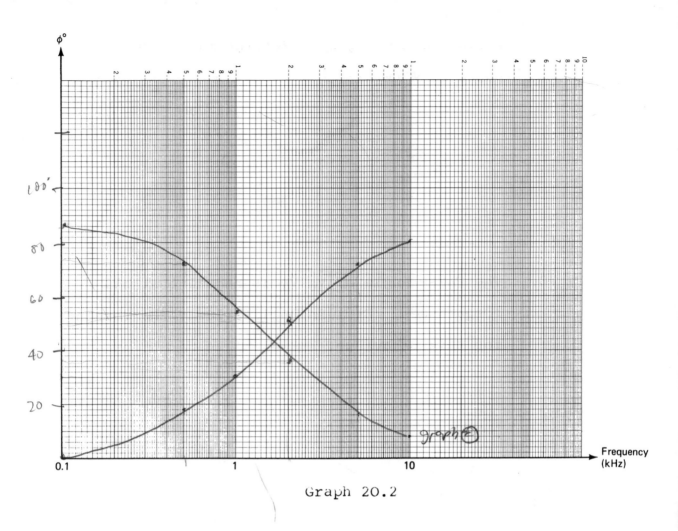

$\phi°$

$100°$

80

60

40

20

0.1   1   10

Frequency (kHz)

graph ⓑ

Graph 20.2

20.5 Comments and Conclusions:

A. Low-Pass Filter:

1. How are the magnitude and phase values
   of V_O/V_T affected by a change in frequency?

2. Suppose that (R) is replaced by (a R), and (C)
   is replaced by (C/a); a is a constant. How

would these changes affect the magnitude and phase of V_O/V_T ?

3. The Phase angle of V_O/V_T is negative at all frequencies. Explain qualitatively the reason for this behaviour.

B. **High-Pass Filter:**

1. How are the magnitude and phase values of V_O/V_T affected by a change in frequency?

2. The phase angle of V_O/V_T is positive at all
    frequencies. Explain (using a phasor diagram)
    the reason for this behaviour.

3. Comment on your results; do your results
    support the theoretical expectations? Explain
    the reasons for possible deviations.

21 GENERAL AC-CIRCUIT: A LOW-PASS BUTTERWORTH FILTER

Required Reading: Text, section 12.5

21.1   **Objective:**

   To examine the frequency response (magnitude and phase) of a simple series-parallel network.

21.2   **Prelab Assignment:**

   Consider the network shown in Fig. 21.1. The network is a second-order low-pass Butterworth filter.

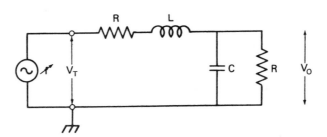

Fig. 21.1

(1) Determine the ratio of V_O/V_T as a function (rad/sec).

(2) Let R = 225 , L = 50 mH and C = 1 μF. Determine the magnitude and phase of V_O/V_T at each of the following frequency settings:

100, 500, 1000, 2000 & 5000 Hz.

(3) Plot the magnitude V_O/V_T and phase ($\phi°$) of V_O/V_T versus frequency on Graphs 21.1 & 21.2, respectively.

Prelab Work Space:

$$\text{teq} \quad \frac{1}{Zeq} = \frac{1}{\frac{1}{j\omega c}} + \frac{1}{R}$$

$$\frac{1}{Zeq} = j\omega c + \frac{1}{R} = \frac{j\omega RC + 1}{R}$$

$$Zeq = \frac{R}{j\omega RC + 1}$$

$$Z_T = R + \omega L + \frac{R}{\omega RC + 1}$$

$$V_T = E \qquad V_0 = \frac{V_T}{Z_T} \cdot Zeq$$

$$= \frac{V_T}{R + \omega L + \frac{R}{\omega RC + 1}} \cdot \frac{R}{\omega RC + 1}$$

$$V_0 = \frac{V_T R}{(R + \omega L)(\omega RC + 1) + R}$$

$$\frac{V_0}{V_T} = \frac{R}{(R + \omega L)(\omega RC + 1) + R}$$

$$= \frac{R}{(R + j\omega L)(j\omega RC + 1)} + 1 = \frac{.225}{}$$

Prelab Work Space:

$f = 100 Hz$ $\dfrac{V_0}{V_T} = 1.768$ $\dfrac{V_0}{V_T} = \dfrac{R}{(R+j\omega L)(\omega RC+1)} + 1$

$\omega = 628.32$

$$= \dfrac{225}{(225 + j\omega 50m)(j\omega(225)(1\mu)+1)} + 1$$

$f = 500 Hz$

$\omega = 3141.6$ $\dfrac{V_0}{V_T} = \dfrac{225}{(225 + j157.08)(1+j0.706)} + 1$ $1.67 \angle 0°$

$f = 1000 Hz$

$\omega = 6283.18$ $\dfrac{V_0}{V_T} = \dfrac{225}{(225 + j314.5)(1+j1.4137)} + 1$ $1.336 \angle 0°$

$f = 2000$

$\omega = 12566.86$ $\dfrac{V_0}{V_T} = \dfrac{225}{(225 + j628.11)(1-j2.827)} + 1 = 1.11 \angle 0°$

$f = 5000$

$\omega = 31415.92$ $\dfrac{V_0}{V_T} = 1.0$ $\dfrac{V_0}{V_T} = \left(\dfrac{R+(R+j\omega L)(\omega RC+1)}{(R+j\omega L)(\omega RC+1)}\right) - 1$

$V_0 = R \cdot \dfrac{1}{}$

$f = 10G$ $\dfrac{V_0}{V_T} = 0.499 \angle -8.1$

500 $= 0.1455 \angle -93.03$ $\dfrac{1}{(R+j\omega L)(j\omega RC+1)}$

1000 $= 0.1356 \angle -80.94$ $\overline{R+(R+j\omega L)(j\omega RC+1)}$

2000 $0.0729 \angle -136.64$ $\dfrac{(R+j\omega L)(j\omega RC+1)}{R} + 1$

5000 $= 0.0203 \angle -163.46$ $j\omega R + 1^2 - \omega^2 LC + \dfrac{j\omega L}{R} + 1$

                               $2 - \omega^2 LC$

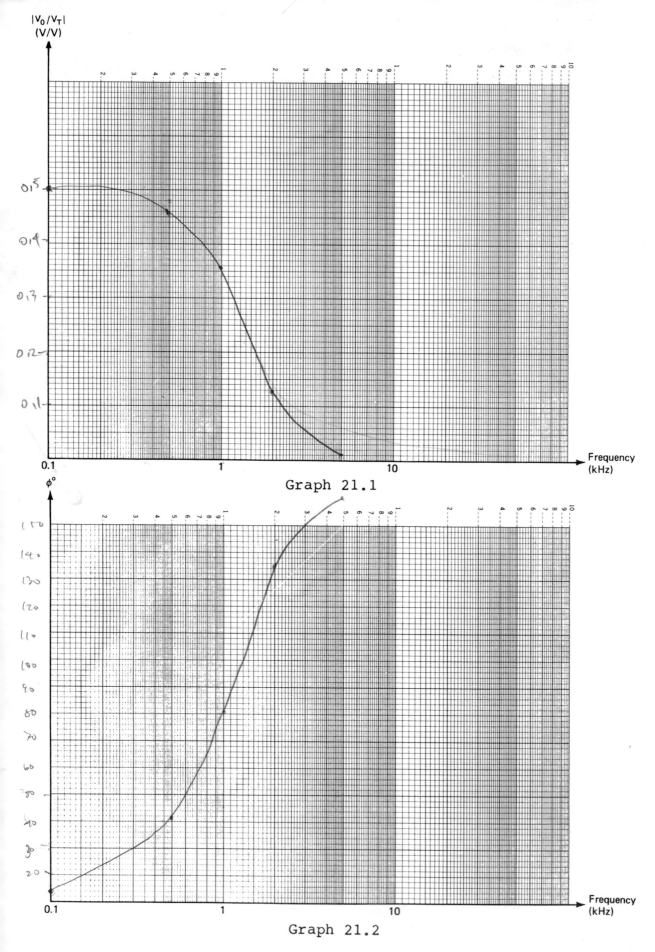

Graph 21.1

Graph 21.2

Equipment:

ITEM	MANUFACTURER AND MODEL NO.	LAB. SERIAL NO
Dual-Beam Oscilloscope		
Signal Generator		
VOM		
Two Decade Resistance Boxes		
Decade Inductance Box		

Capacitors: One 1μ F

21.4   **Procedure:**

(1)   Adjust the decade inductance box to 50 mH
      and use the VOM to measure its internal
      resistance r_L. $r_L = 130\Omega$

(2)   Connect the circuit shown in Fig. 21.2.
      Adjust R_1 to 225 Ω and R_2 to $(225 - r_L)\Omega$.

      $R2 = 95\Omega$

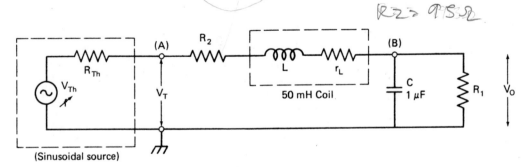

Fig. 21.2

233

(3) Use channel Y_A of the oscilloscope to
     display V_T; adjust V_T (p-p) to 10V at
     100 Hz. [V_T must be maintained at
     10V (p-p) for all the following frequency
     settings.]

(4) Use Y_B to display V_O. Measure V_O (p-p)
     and the phase angle ($\phi°$) of V_O w.r.t. V_T
     [See Section 16.6]. Determine the ratio of
     $\dfrac{V_O \text{ (p-p)}}{V_T \text{ (p-p)}}$, and record your results in Table
     21.1.

(5) Repeat the above set of measurements for each
     frequency setting in Table 21.1.

Table 21.1

Frequency (Hz)	$\dfrac{V_O \ (p\text{-}p)}{V_T \ (p\text{-}p)}$ (V/V)	$\phi°$ (degrees)
100	$\dfrac{5.1}{10} = 0.51$	$1.23°$ 3
150	$\dfrac{5.1}{10} = 0.51$	$5.625°$
250	$\dfrac{5.0}{10} = 0.15$	$7.34°$
350	$\dfrac{4.8}{10} = 0.48$	$12.13°$
500	$\dfrac{4.7}{10} = 0.47$	$15°$
700	$4.5/10 = 0.45$	$25.7°$
800	$4.3/10 = 0.43$	$30°$
1000	$\dfrac{4.1}{10} = 0.41$	$36°$
1500	$3.9/10 = 0.39$	$46.45°$
2000	$3.0/10 = 0.30$	$53.6°$
3000	$2.5/10 = 0.25$	$63.87°$
3500	$1.9/10 = 0.19$	$66.67°$
4000	$1.7/10 = 0.17$	$67.2°$
5000	$1.4/10 = 0.14$	$6.75°$
6000	$1.2/10 = 0.12$	$6418°$
8500	$0.9/10 = 0.09$	$75°$

(6)   Plot V_O/V_T and ($\phi°$) versus frequency on

Graphs 21.1 & 21.2, respectively.

235

Comments and Conclusions:

1. How are the magnitude and phase

    of V_O/V_T affected by a change in frequency?

2. The phase angle of V_O/V_T is negative at
    all frequencies. Explain qualitatively
    the reason for this behaviour.

3. Draw the phasor diagram for the voltage of
    each node (w.r.t. ground) and the current
    through each branch at 1000 Hz.

4. Repeat Question # 3 for f = 10 kHz. What are the major differences between the two phasor diagrams at 1 k and 10 kHz?

22 | THE TRANSFORMER

Required Reading: Text, section 17.5 and 17.6

22.1   **Objective:**

To understand the basic principles of transformers.

22.2   A.   **Background:**

A transformer is a device that transfers electrical energy from one circuit to another by electromagnetic induction. Transformers need very little care and maintenance. They can vary in size from a very large stationary device such as a power transformer to miniature components using only a few windings and with air as the core material.

Transformers are more commonly used to step-up or step-down voltages. They are also frequently used to electrically isolate electronic equipment from the ac power source or isolate one part of the circuit from the other; these transformers are called 'isolation transformers'. Transformers are also used in some electronic circuits to match the impedance of the load to the source impedance.

Transformers are primarily classified according to their usage such as audio, power, radio frequency, modulation and filament transformers. They can also be classified according to the type and shape of the core material used.

The typical transformer has two windings: a 'primary' which is connected to the source and a 'secondary' across which the load is connected. They are wound on a common magnetic core and insulated from each other electrically.

The following relationships are valid under ideal operating conditions of transformers:

$$\frac{V_p}{V_s} = \frac{I_s}{I_p} = \frac{N_p}{N_s} = a$$

where, 'a' is the transformation or turns ratio.

The impedance of the secondary circuit reflected to the primary side is determined from:

$$Z_p = a^2 Z_s$$

The equation above can be used to calculate the turns ratio required to match the reflected impedance of the load to the source impedance.

B.   **Prelab Assignment:**

(1)   A transformer rated at 50 volt-amps,

120V (Primary)/50V (Secondary), is connected

to a 60 Hz AC source with a terminal voltage

of 20 Volts RMS.   Calculate:

$\dfrac{120}{150} = \dfrac{I_s}{I_p}$

$\dfrac{120}{150} = \dfrac{1}{\alpha}$

(a)   the primary and secondary currents when

a load resistance of 50 Ω is connected

across the secondary winding.

(b)   the number of turns on the secondary

winding if the primary winding has

720 turns.

(c)   the RMS current in the primary winding if

a resistive load of 500 Ω is connected

across the secondary; determine the

value of the resistance reflected to the

primary side.

(d)   the reflected impedance if a load of

10 μ F capacitor in series with 200 Ω

resistance is connected across the

secondary winding.

(2)   Assume that the above transformer has a

center-tapped secondary winding and a load

of 50 Ω connected as shown in Fig. 22.1.

Calculate:

(a)   the RMS values of V_s, I_p and I_s,

(b) 'a' and Z_p.

(c) Volt-Ampere (input) and Volt-Ampere (Output).

Record your results in Table 22.2.

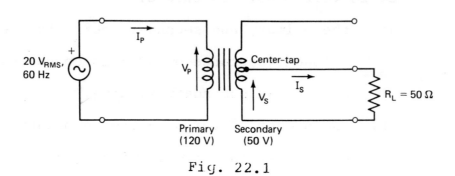

Fig. 22.1

Prelab Work Space:

Prelab Work Space:

ITEM	MANUFACTURER AND MODEL NO.	LAB. SERIAL NO
Signal Generator		
DMM or VOM		
AC Milliammeter		
Decade Resistance Box		
Transformer		

Capacitors: 10 μ F

22.4   Procedure:

(1)   Connect the circuit shown in Fig. 22.2.
Adjust the terminal voltage of the AC source
to 20V RMS at 60 Hz.

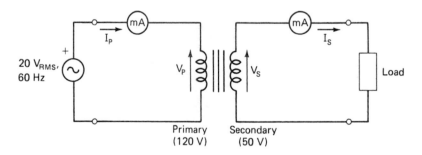

Fig. 22.2

(2)   For the various values of the loads shown in
      Table 22.1, measure the RMS values of
      V_p, V_s, I_p and I_s.   Record the results in
      Table 22.1.

Table 22.1

Load	V_p (V)	V_s (V)	I_p (mA)	I_s (mA)	$\dfrac{V_p}{V_s}$	$\dfrac{I_s}{I_p}$	Z_p (Ω)	Z_s (Ω)
Open-Circuit								
R_L = 1 kΩ								
R_L = 500 Ω								
R_L = 100 Ω								
R_L = 50 Ω								
10 μ F in Series with 200 Ω								

(3)   Connect the circuit shown in Fig. 22.3.

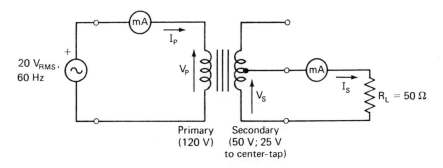

Fig. 22.3

Measure the RMS values of V_p, V_s, I_s and I_p.
Record the results in Table 22.2 and
calculate 'a', Z_p, Volt-Ampere (input) and
Volt-Ampere (output).

Table 22.2

	V_p (V)	V_s (V)	I_p (mA)	I_s (mA)	$a = \dfrac{V_p}{V_s}$	Z_p (Ω)	(VA) IN	(VA) OUT
CALC. Prelab.								
Measured								

22.5   **Comments and Conclusions:**

1.   Did the measured values of the transformation
ratio [as determined by the voltage and
current measurements in Table 22.2] match
the name plate ratio of transformation? If
not, what are the possible reasons?

2. Do the values of Z_p calculated (for $R_L=50\,\Omega$) in Tables 22.1 and 22.2 equal the corresponding values of a^2Z_s? If not, explain why.

3. What conclusions can you draw from the power calculations in Table 22.2?

4. If a transformer is required to be used as an isolation transformer only, what should be the ratio of transformation (a)?

5. What is the 'rated' secondary current of your transformer if it is used as:

   (a) a step-up transformer,

   (b) a step-down transformer?